SHOUT FOR THE VICTORY

Scepter of Favor Ministries
P.O. Box 2346
Rolla, MO 65402

SHOUT FOR THE VICTORY

By
Judith A. Reno

Cover Design: Brad Graber

Companion Press
P.O. Box 351
Shippensburg, PA 17257-0351

ISBN 1-56043-472-4

For Worldwide Distribution
Printed in the U.S.A.

Table of Contents

Prayer

Dear Father in Heaven, I humbly come before your throne of grace to ask you to bless those who read the pages of this book. Father, may you anoint this book by the power of your Holy Spirit. May each person receive new revelation and understanding of your Word. May your Holy Spirit teach, comfort and encourage them. May faith in your Word be increased as they read. Lord may your children learn to love you, to praise you, to bless you, to shout praises to you, even in the midst of trials and difficult circumstances.

Send forth the Holy Spirit with each book to work in power in the minds and hearts of every reader. May there be breakthroughs and victories won in each life. Let each reader rise to a new level of overcoming in their lives as they began shouting for the victory!

May all power and glory and honor be unto you for ever and ever! In the precious and wonderful name of Jesus I ask these things.

Amen,
Judith

Dedication

This book is lovingly dedicated to the Lord Jesus Christ, my best friend, for the encouragement He has continually given me to write this book. Without Him I truly could not have accomplished such a task. He knows I'm not a writer! The Holy Spirit did a great job of encouraging me to finish what I had started. Thank you precious Lord that through you we can do all things!

A special thank-you also to my second best friend, Fred, my husband, for his help and encouragement. Also to my daughters, Jennifer and Christie, for their love and support. My son-in-law, Brad, for allowing the Lord to use his talents to design the cover. And to my dear friend, Bruce Jubanowsky for editing the book.

Preface

In 1983 the Lord gave me revelation on the power of shouting high praises to God. As I studied and began to teach on this subject the Lord continued to give me more revelation.

I am convinced that we are in a battle, and that our battle is with principalities and powers of darkness. It is my desire that all Christians everywhere learn to live in victory over these evil forces. It is out of this desire that I have been led to write a book on the subject of "shouting."

Shouting is a very effective weapon used in spiritual warfare. I have not only seen breakthroughs in my life through using this weapon, but in the lives of others. I have been teaching on this subject for seven years and have had untold numbers of people ask me to write a book. When I teach on this subject, there are always fruits in people's lives. Many people have told me their testimonies of how shouting has caused them to get victory in the midst of trials when nothing else worked.

The shout was used throughout the Old Testament as a means of warfare. It was the shout that brought down the walls of Jericho. It was the shout that sent

Jehoshaphat's enemies into utter confusion, and took the children of Israel into ultimate victory. In the very beginning of time, when God created the earth, we are told that its foundations were brought forth with shoutings (Job 38). God told Zerubbabel "not by might nor by power, but by My Spirit...and you shall bring forth the capstones with shouts of 'Grace, grace to it!'" (Zech. 3:7) When David brought up the Ark of the Covenant of the Lord, he brought it forth with loud shoutings, and with the sound of the horn, with trumpets, with loud-sounding cymbals, with harps and lyres. (1 Cron. 15:28) And we are told that Jesus would return to the earth with a "shout!"

God is restoring the shout of victory to the body of Christ in these last days. He wants this message taught to the whole body of Christ. I believe that is why He has led me to write on the subject. The shout of victory will be an instrumental tool for all Christians to encourage them to allow the high praises of God to be on their lips and flow freely from deep within their hearts.

Foreword

This book is a vital tool for every believer who wishes to live as an overcomer. We are living in a day when the battle is raging round about us. Time is running short and satan is on the rampage. Many believers are under severe attack by enemy forces. In the natural, life may appear bleak and gloomy—like there is no hope, no way out. BUT—PRAISE GOD—as believers we are not limited to what we see with our natural eye! God has already rescued us from the dominion of darkness and translated us into His kingdom of light. Our Father has provided abundant life for all who would believe and receive.

Though the intensity of the war is increasing and you may feel you are in the heat of the battle, you don't have to live a downtrodden, defeated life of despair. The book that you are holding in your hands offers a wealth of practical, spiritual guidelines, supported by scripture, which, if applied to your own life, will cause you to rise up and soar above all adversity! **SHOUT FOR THE VICTORY** is a book of substance and will provoke you to take your rightful place of triumph. Why be overcome by the circumstances of life here on this earth when you can "shout for the victory" and rise to new heights in God's kingdom!?!

Shalom and Love,
Sid Roth

Introduction

There is a battle taking place today all around us. It is not a battle you can see with your eyes, but an unseen battle in the spiritual realm. As we come closer to the second coming of Jesus Christ, the battle gets more intense.

In Ephesians 6 we are told that we wrestle not against flesh and blood but against principalities and powers and spiritual forces of evil in high places. Therefore, we are to put on the whole armor of God and fight the good fight of faith. A fight is only a good fight when we **win the battle!**

In this book I will tell about a mighty weapon we can use for the pulling down of evil strongholds. It is not the only weapon we must use as a Christian soldier, but it is an important one in winning the battle. This weapon needs to be restored to the army of God as we go into battle, so that we don't lose any more battles before we win the war.

Our weapon is shouting high praises to God! As we learn to "Shout for the Victory," we will see the mountains become as plains, the walls of many strongholds tumble around the deceiver, and God arrive on the scene and cause His enemies to BE SCATTERED!

God has established His Church upon the revealed truth of Jesus Christ and has promised that the gates of hell shall **not** BE ABLE TO STAND UP AGAINST IT! Every weapon in God's arsenal is required for battle, and too often, shouting has been overlooked as a powerful means of attack and defense.

Let us not go into battle ill-equipped nor unprepared. We must take on **all** our mighty weapons. As the army of God marches toward our final battle, let us SHOUT FOR THE VICTORY!

I

Why Fight?

Early in my Christian walk with the Lord, before I had ever heard any teachings on the power of praise, I had an experience of overcoming sickness through singing and shouting praises.

It was "flu" season and most of my friends and neighbors had come down with a terrible case of the flu. Before becoming a Christian, I always caught anything that was going around! So it was natural to believe that I would continue in this pattern.

I happened to be in my car driving when I began aching all over my body. As the minutes passed, I started feeling nauseated. The feelings of dread flooded me as I thought, "Oh, no, I'm coming down with the same flu that everyone else has." Suddenly another thought interrupted **"just ignore it and sing praises!"**

Being a new born Christian, I only knew a couple of songs. But I gently began singing "The Joy of the Lord is my Strength." At first it was very difficult. I could barely get the words out. I felt as though I was going to throw-up at any moment. Thoughts raced through my head as I sang: "you had better pull over to the side of the road and get out of your car; you're sick and any moment the whole car will be dirty!"

However something inside me kept saying, "no, ignore it and sing." I continued singing, "The Joy of the Lord is my Strength" over and over. Soon I began feeling stronger and stronger. The symptoms started leaving and it occurred to me that I was being delivered from the flu. I started laughing and shouting, "Hallelujah, hallelujah, Praise you Lord, Praise you Lord!" Arriving home, still singing and rejoicing, I felt perfectly fine. All symptoms had disappeared!

That was sixteen years ago. It seemed like a small incident at the time. But actually God was beginning to teach me not to accept every sickness that came along. I had no idea of the battles I would face in the future and that I was in training, being prepared for war!

Since the fall of man in the Garden of Eden there has been a war raging. The war is in the spiritual realm. It is an unseen war, but it is just as real as anything that can be seen with the natural eyes. This battle is light against darkness, good against evil, righteousness against unrighteousness, courage versus fear, God against satan. When we **choose** God, we have chosen to be on His side of the battle, and God's enemies become our enemies. Thus, when we became a child of God, we were automatically "enlisted" in God's army. And being on His side, we became engaged in spiritual warfare. We can ignore it, not admit it, or even deny it, but the fact remains we **will** encounter our mutual enemy—the devil and his cohorts.

Many Christians believe, as I used to, that satan is God's opposite. However it just is not true. You see, God has **no** opposites! He is the **only** All-Knowing One. He is the **only** All-Seeing One. He is the **only** All-Powerful One. There is no one like Him. For it is written:

I am the Lord, and there is none else; There is no God beside Me. (Isa. 45:5a, KJV)

God is the **only God!** There is no other like Him! **HE IS THE ALMIGHTY ONE,** and He has no **opposites!** Satan is not God's opposite, but satan does have an opposite. Satan's opposite is Michael the Archangel and Gabriel. When we realize this truth we will be able to understand just how defeated satan really is! His only weapons are to deceive us, to get us to believe his lies, and to cause us to react in fear so that he may overcome us. Satan builds his strongholds up in our minds. Once we believe his lies that exalt themselves against the knowledge of God's truth, we have fallen into one of his traps!

God's will for us is that we overcome satan's attacks and his schemes in **every** area of our lives. He has given us the ability to **always** triumph through Jesus Christ. But we must **choose** to "put on" the full armor of God daily and fight, or we will be defeated. As warriors we have been given the power and authority to destroy the works of the devil in our lives, in our families' lives, and in the lives of those with whom God has knit us together in the body of Christ. Jesus came to destroy the works of the devil, and he was victorious; now we, being His body, can enter into that victory! Jesus, being the head, isn't going to do anything without us who are His body. Because we are a part of one another, what the head does, the body will do also. Everything Jesus has already accomplished we now have the ability to accomplish through Him.

When the devil comes as a thief to steal, to kill, and to destroy, if we do not do anything about it, we will surely live defeated Christian lives. Why? Because the Word says we will! The Scripture admonishes:

If you remain indifferent in the time of adversity, your strength will depart from you. (Prov. 24:10, NAB)

For example, if Russia was sending missiles to America, and America remained indifferent about it, her strength would depart. If someone is fighting against you, and you do not do anything about it, you will be overcome and defeated!

We have become engaged in spiritual warfare. The Holy Spirit tells us through Paul:

For we are not fighting against people made of flesh and blood, but against persons without bodies—the evil rulers of the unseen world, those mighty satanic beings and great evil princes of darkness who rule this world; and against huge numbers of wicked spirits in the spirit world. (Eph. 6:12, LB)

4

In other words, when we are encountering problems and trials, it may look like it is people and circumstances that we are up against. It could be a relationship problem, health problem, financial problem, or some other problem. But here God is saying, it's not what it looks like to our natural eyes; our problem is really a spiritual one. There are powers and principalities of wickedness, satan and his demons, who are really **behind** the problem.

When someone is fighting in the natural, for example, he is in the ring boxing or wrestling. He isn't just sitting there thinking about it. He is not running away from it. No, he is actually **doing** something physical about it. He is fighting, which takes A LOT of strength and endurance. Now God has not said "meditate on it." He has not said "flee" from it. No, He said to "fight." That is why we are told to put on the whole armor of God and to fight the good fight of faith. God would not tell us to fight unless there was a reason to fight. We are to fight because of the enemy who comes to **kill**, to **steal**, and to **destroy** (John 10:10, KJV). Examine these words...

To **KILL** means to make you die, to put an end to you, to stop you, to prevent you from going forward. To destroy your vital and active qualities.[1]

To **STEAL** means to rob you, in secret, without your even knowing you have been robbed! To take something that belongs to you. To steal implies robbery performed in

---

1.   *Webster's Dictionary*

secret.[2] You might not even be aware that something has been taken from you!

To **DESTROY** means to tear down, to demolish, to break up or spoil completely, to ruin, to bring to total defeat, to crush, to do away with, to neutralize the effect of, to make you **useless!**[3]

God tells us "to fight **hard** for the faith" in Jude 1:3 (NAB).

I Pet. 5:8-9a (NAS) says:

*Be of sober spirit, be on the alert. Your adversary, the devil, prowls about like a roaring lion, seeking someone to devour. But **resist** him, firm in your faith, knowing that the same experiences of suffering are being accomplished by your own brethren in the world.*

The Amplified Bible makes it even stronger when it says;

*Be well-balanced, temperate, sober-minded; be vigilant and cautious at all times, for that enemy of yours, the devil, roams around like a lion roaring [in fierce hunger], seeking someone to seize upon and devour. **Withstand** him, be firm in faith [against his onset,]—rooted, established, strong, immovable and determined,—knowing that the same [identical] sufferings are appointed to your*

---

2.   *Webster's Dictionary*
3.   *Webster's Dictionary*

brotherhood [the whole body of Christians] throughout the world.

Resist means to withstand; oppose, fend off, stand firm against, withstand the action of, to oppose actively, fight, argue, or work against, **to refuse to submit to.**[4]

To **withstand** means to oppose, resist, or endure, especially in a successful way. We are told to:

Withstand him, be firm in faith against his onset— rooted, established, strong, immoveable and determined—knowing that the same (identical) sufferings are appointed to your brotherhood (the whole body of Christians) throughout the world. (1 Pet. 5:9, AMP)

Withstanding satan means we are to actively oppose him. We are to refuse to submit to him, and to fight hard against him, firmly resisting his actions. We must obey the Word of God if we expect to receive the promises of God. If we don't withstand satan we **will** be defeated!

All Christians go through trials, but **not** all Christians live victorious lives. We make the decision whether to fight or not to fight, and our **decision determines whether we will overcome or be overcome.** God **never** lies! He has promised that if we fight the good fight of faith, He will **always** cause us to triumph through Christ.

---

4.   *Webster's Dictionary*

It is important to remember that we are on the Victor's side. We have the potential within us to overcome in every area of our life because God is on our side. With God on our side, how can we ever be defeated? For He always causes us to triumph when we are living in union with Christ Jesus.

All the powers and principalities of darkness were conquered when Jesus took the keys of the kingdom from satan and stripped him of his power. He then gave **us** as believers power and authority over **all** the powers of the enemy, and nothing shall by any means ever hurt us. As God's representatives, we have been given the power and authority to "bind" (to stop) as well as the authority to "loose" (to allow). Mt. 18:18 (AMP) says:

Truly, I tell you, whatever you forbid and declare to be improper and unlawful on earth must be what is already forbidden in heaven, and whatever you permit and declare proper and lawful on earth must be already permitted in heaven.

In heaven, all evil is forbidden. All sorrow, pain, hurt and suffering is forbidden, but what **is** permitted is love, peace, joy and all the other fruits of the Holy Spirit. We have power, and we have authority over all the powers of the enemy, but **unused** power and authority will accomplish nothing. God has given us the power and authority to forbid anything that is forbidden in heaven. If we do not take the authority and use it, it will not be of any benefit to us. When Jesus was getting ready to leave the earth, He gave His followers all rights to use His name and His power. He said:

All authority—all power of rule—in heaven and on earth has been given Me. (Mt. 28:18, AMP)

Then, Jesus commissioned His followers to go in His name and in His authority. He said that in His name we would do even greater works than He had done.

And He said to them, go into all the world and preach and publish openly the good news (Gospel) to every creature (of the whole human race). He who believes (that is), who adheres to and trusts in and relies on the Gospel and Him whom it sets forth and is baptized will be saved (from the penalty of eternal death); but he who does not believe—who does not adhere to and trust in and rely on the Gospel and Him whom sets it forth—will be condemned. And these attesting signs will accompany those who believe; In My name they will drive out demons; they will speak in new languages; they will pick up serpents, and (even) if they drink anything deadly, it will not hurt them; they will lay their hands on the sick, and they will get well. (Mark 16:15, AMP)

*And Jesus came and spoke unto them, saying, **all authority** is given to me in heaven and on earth. Go ye therefore and teach all nations, baptizing them in the name of the Father, and of the Son, and of the Holy Ghost. Teaching them to observe all things whatsoever I have commanded you, and lo, I*

*am with you always, even to the end of the world.
Amen.* (Matt. 28:18, KJV)

God had given Adam and Eve "authority" over the whole earth. He told them to take dominion over the earth and to subdue it. Adam and Eve choose not to obey God and instead gave in to the lies of the serpent and obeyed him. What they should have done is to take authority over him and rebuke his lies. However, because of their disobedience they lost their authority over the earth and became a slave to it instead. In essence, they sold their right of authority to the devil. The devil then became the "ruler" or "god" of this world.

When Jesus came to earth, He paid the price for man's rebellion by submitting his own life to the will of God, even though it meant His death. Through the obedience of Jesus to the will of the Father, Jesus paid the price to take back the dominion or "authority" from the devil. Had the rulers of this world known the plan of God, they would never have crucified Jesus. But in God's great plan of salvation He knew that through the death of His Son, man would once again be able to take dominion over the earth, the devil, and his demons. Jesus took the keys of the kingdom away from satan and He gave them to the children of God.

Now we are told that God has put all things in **subjection** under man's feet. (Heb. 2:7) In other words, God is telling His people that we have the authority to control or rule over the earth. But we must take that authority and use it or it will not do us any good. The word "subjection" means to be placed under the control of. God has put all things under the control of man's feet.

As Christians, we at least should have our own lives and bodies under the control of our spirit and have victory within ourselves. As we are walking in righteousness and have our bodies under control, we will be able to take authority over the devil. Then we should be able to help others in trouble.

Paul not only understood the importance of authority, but He tells us that He **took control** of his body;

> But [like a boxer] I buffet my body—handle it roughly, discipline it by hardships—and **subdue** it, for fear that after proclaiming to others the Gospel and things pertaining to it, I myself should become unfit—not stand the test and be unapproved—and rejected [as a counterfeit]. (1 Cor. 9:27, AMP)

Paul took authority over fleshly desires that were not pleasing to God, and he subjected his body to his spirit. God has given all His children the ability to make their bodies subject to their spirits. But if we do not take that authority and **do** something about it, our bodies will be the one in control instead of our spirit. For we are told that the flesh wars against the spirit and the spirit wars against the flesh. We are the ones who determine who will win.

The more we submit to the authority of God's Word in our lives, the more authority we will have. We have the choice every day of walking in the spirit or letting the flesh take control. God has already given us the authority. Now we have to use it in order to walk in the spirit.

The reason Jesus has given us His authority is because He knew we would **need** it. He walked and lived in the earth, and He was quite aware of the fact that there was a spiritual battle taking place in the heavenlies. Jesus knew that we would need His power and His authority in order to be able to overcome the evil forces in the earth. That is why He has given us His authority and power.

So, why fight? Because we are in a spiritual battle, and if we do not fight in the battle, we will be overcome by the problems and trials; we will live defeated Christian lives. God wants an overcoming Church. He desires a obedient, strong, courageous, victorious overcoming bride that will be a glory to Him. He wants a bride whom He can look at and be proud of—a beautiful victorious bride without spot or wrinkle. A people chosen by Him, a people called apart, a strong fearless people, who will rule and reign with Him when He returns to earth.

We were enlisted in God's army when we were born again into His Kingdom. Now we are to be good soldiers of the Lord Jesus Christ. We are commanded to be strong and faithful to God. The **purpose** for an army is to fight in battle. We will either be fighting or retreating until we go home to be with the Lord. Until then we need to be on the offensive, not the defensive. If we wait until we are on the defensive, it will be much more difficult to win the battle.

In the recent war that was fought in the Middle East, our nation was on the offensive. We didn't attack just one time, no, we attacked day and night relentlessly until we were certain the battle was won. We never stopped fighting until we knew we had the victory.

If we, as Christian Soldiers, stay on the offensive against our enemy and relentlessly go forward possessing the land for our God, we will see many more children born into the Kingdom of God. We will have less casualties and more victories.

The Old Testament was written for our instruction and our learning by the examples of those who lived before us. It is full of examples of war and warfare. God did not have the Holy Spirit anoint the prophets of old to write about fighting for no purpose. It was so that we would be equipped to fight and understand spiritual warfare. The Word of God mentions "armor" and "weapons" many times. Rom. 13:12 talks about the "armor" of light; 2 Cor. 6:7 talks about, the "weapons" of righteousness. In Eph. 6 we are told to put on the "full armor of God."

We would not need "armor" or "weapons" unless there was a battle going on! We are in a battle even though we don't see it with our natural eyes. It is imperative that we keep our armor on and fight with the weapons God has given us. Not only do we need to fight, but we need to stand in faith believing in the truthfulness of the Word of God.

When I was a young Christian, I was attending classes every week teaching about the power of God's Word to

13

heal. As I learned the Word of God concerning healing my faith to be healed began to grow. At the time I was on sulfur tablets due to a long-standing kidney problem. The medication had a side effect that made me very nauseated. However, my doctor had said that I had to stay on this drug for the rest of my life, and could not stop taking the medicine without serious complications.

One day I heard the Lord speak to me about the problem. He told me to discontinue the medication and believe Him for healing. I was led by the Holy Spirit to get rid of the medicine. He told me to stand on the promise in Isaiah 53, "By whose stripes you were healed", and to thank Him every day for healing me.

Little did I know what a battle I faced for the next year! The symptoms of the kidney disease would come and go. Many times I had blood in my urine and was doubled up with pain. There were times when the devil came and attacked me with a spirit of fear and thoughts of death. No matter how bad the circumstances got, I stood on the promise of God and thanked Him that I was healed, calling those things that were not as though they were.

Finally, one day as my husband and I were preparing a testimony to share at our Church, the following day, I began to have the most severe pain with bleeding that I had ever experienced. Fear immediately gripped me. I went to my husband and told him about the severe pain and bleeding I had. My faith was wavering as I began to think back to the warnings of my doctor. However, my husband, realizing that this was a spiritual battle, just looked at me and grabbed my hands. He began shouting praises to God thanking Him that I was healed. A righteous holy anger rose up on the inside of us as we rebuked satan and his lying symptoms. We were so angry at the devil that we attacked him violently! At the time, we knew very little about taking authority or about the power of high praises. However, the Spirit of the Lord on the inside of us, who knows all things, rose up against our enemy. The Word of God declares, "Let God arise and His enemies be scattered". And that is exactly what happened to us that day! The symptoms left the next day and from that day to this I have been healed of the kidney disease! Praise the Lord forever!

Now, I want you to realize that I am in **no** way telling you to stop taking your medication if you are under the authority of a doctor. No, I believe God uses doctors to help us get well. God uses medicine to help us get rid of diseases. All good things come from God. But do you know that if God didn't help you, even the medicine wouldn't work!

How many times have you had a sickness and been given medication from a doctor? Now, tell me the truth, didn't you begin to feel better right away? As soon as you took that first pill, you began to **believe** that you were going to get better. Your faith in healing had increased, and God used the medication to help heal you.

However, if the Lord speaks to you and tells you to believe Him for healing, and to stop taking your medication, you need to obey Him. That doesn't necessarily mean that you won't have to fight in order to get the victory.

If I hadn't fought, then I would have remained sick. It took me over a year of believing God's Word, confessing it and thanking God for healing me before all the symptoms were totally gone. I wasn't healed instantly. My faith and patience were severely tested during that year. However, I never gave up! Thank God that I had a husband who would stand with me and agree with me in prayer.

There are times when our faith might waver, that is when we need to get reinforcement troops to help us. An army consists of many soldiers. Some are experts in different fields. When we are growing tired and weary, we need to ask others who are stronger to assist us in fighting the battle. In any warfare there will most likely be some wounded soldiers and even some casualties. But that doesn't mean that we should give up the fight.

Fighting is not easy, it is not something that brings a lot of joy while doing it. Fighting is often difficult and hard work. But when we win the fight, when we see the victory, and see our enemy defeated, that is when the joy comes; that is when we can look back and say, "Well, thank God I fought! Thank God I did not give up during the heat of the battle. Praise the Lord that through His power and strength I have won this battle and it was well worth the fighting!"

II

Taking the Kingdom by Force

Jesus said in Luke 10:19 (KJV):

*Behold, I give unto you power to tread on serpents
and scorpions and over **all** the power of the enemy
and nothing shall by any means hurt you.*

Notice, He gave **us** the power over the enemy. **We** are
now the ones responsible. Jesus gave us the "power of at-
torney," so to speak, and now we must **do** something
about it. We must be a doer of the word and not a hearer
only. We need to take our authority and use it. The word
"authority" means "the power or right to give commands,
enforce obedience, take action, or make final decisions;
the position of having such power".[1]

We need to stand strong and declare, "I forbid that in
Jesus' name." We have authority! Now we need to use it!

---

1.   *Webster's Dictionary*

The kind of authority that God is talking about here is not one of strength in the flesh, but the kind of authority that a policeman has. A policeman may have limited strength as far as his physical body is concerned to stop heavy cars in traffic. You see, his authority is given to him by a higher authority, and he has the legal right to make people obey lawful commands when the situation demands it. He can command the traffic to stop when he wants it to stop. In the same way a believer has legal authority given him by God. It is a legal right of every believer to be able to take authority over demons. But just because we have authority over demons does not mean that we will never have to fight in God's kingdom. We must enforce the authority that has been given to us by God.

We read in Mt. 11:12 (AMP):

And from the days of John the Baptist until the present time the kingdom of heaven has endured violent assault, and violent men seize it by force (as a precious prize)—a share in the heavenly kingdom is sought for with most ardent zeal and intense exertion.

Notice we are told at this present time that the kingdom of God is suffering **VIOLENT ASSAULT**! The word violence means "physical force used so as to injure, damage, or destroy; extreme roughness of action, intense, often devastatingly or explosively powerful force or energy as of a hurricane or volcano; unjust or callous use of force or power, as in violating another's rights; vehement fury."[2] Now let us read this scripture from the King James version:

And from the days of John the Baptist until now the kingdom of heaven suffereth violence and the violent take it by force.

We are told that God's kingdom on earth suffers violence! What is God saying here? Well, God has a kingdom here on earth; He also has one in heaven. God's perfect will is being done in heaven, that is why we are told to pray that His will would be done on earth as it is in heaven. You see, in heaven, God's perfect will **is** done. We are told that in heaven there is no sin, no sickness, no sorrow, or evil. There is peace, joy and love. However, God says that on earth His kingdom suffers violence and is extremely damaged and injured unjustly by the evil one. But God does not stop there. He continues by saying: "THE VIOLENT TAKE IT BY FORCE!" There is a violent war raging in the heavenlies. We cannot see it, but we can see the destructive evidence in people's lives if we have the eyes to see. Do not be deceived into sitting back and allowing things just to happen in your life.

In order for God's will to be accomplished on earth, we must force it to (or make it) happen through our perseverance and fervent prayers. We are going to have to become **violent** in our prayers in order to force God's will in our lives and the lives of others. God's will is not just

---

2.   *Webster's Dictionary*

automatically done on this earth. No, many things happen that are against the will of God. That is why Jesus told us to pray for His will to be done on earth as it is in heaven. If God's will were done there would not be sin, sickness or anything else evil done here on earth. It was **not** God's will for Adam and Eve to sin. It is **never** God's will for mankind to sin.

However, God has created us in His image, and we have our own free will. God will never violate our right to control our own will. He might allow circumstances to be so difficult at times that we give up our will and surrender to His will, especially for those who are His children. But when we truly surrender our lives to the lordship of Jesus Christ, we pray as Jesus Himself did: "Father, not my will but Yours be done in my life." You see, The Father always knows what is best for us even when we do not know what is best.

But we **do** know what the Bible tells us **is** God's will in heaven and what is happening in heaven. In heaven there is no hatred, no gossip, no slander, no criticism, no sin, no sickness, no evil of any kind. In heaven there is peace, love, joy and happiness. In heaven everyone loves and worships God.

The Lord's desire is for us to bring about His will on earth as it is in heaven. We can do this through our prayers. We are instructed to **persevere in prayer**, and to **pray without ceasing**. To persevere in prayer means to continue to pray in spite of difficulty or opposition. To refuse to relent or quit, especially in the face of opposition or interference. To keep on praying stubbornly **refusing** to give up.

To pray without ceasing means that all day long while we are working, etc., we should be continually praying about everything. To pray without ceasing means to **not stop** but to keep praying **all the time**. We can pray in the spirit even while we are talking to someone. We should pray all the time, about everything without stopping or giving up.

Many times we give up when things look hopeless and we lose our faith and get into doubt which leads to unbelief. Doubt and unbelief will cause us to lose the battle.

All too often we let up when we start to see the victory, and don't **continue to persevere** for a complete victory. This opens the door for the devil to re-enter the fight. When that happens it weakens our faith and we have to start all over again. A good example of not giving up is in the parable of the Syrophoenician woman in Mt. 15:21-28 (NAS):

> *And Jesus went away from there, and withdrew into the district of Tyre and Sidon. And behold, a Canaanite woman came out from that region, and began to **cry out**, saying, "Have mercy on me, O Lord, Son of David; my daughter is cruelly demon-possessed." **But He did not answer her a word.** And his disciples came to Him and kept asking Him, saying, "Send her away, for she is **shouting** out after us." But He answered and said, "I was sent only to the lost sheep of the house of Israel." But she*

came and began to bow down before Him, saying, "Lord, help me!" And He answered and said, "It is not good to take the children's bread and throw it to the dogs." But she said, "Yes, Lord, but even the dogs feed on the crumbs which fall from their masters' table." Then Jesus answered and said to her, "O woman, your faith is great; be it done for you as you wish." And her daughter was healed at once.

Notice in this story how persistent this woman was. Even when Jesus would not speak to her she did not give up. When Jesus, in fact, was saying **"no"** to her, she continued to believe and persevere in asking Him to heal her daughter. We read that she was "crying out" to the Lord and "shouting" out at His disciples. To make matters worse the disciples complain about her to Jesus and tell Him to send her away. Talk about rejection, first by the fact that Jesus didn't speak to her and then she was rejected by His disciples! Jesus tells her "no" a **second** time when He said, "It is not good to take children's bread and throw it to the dogs." Still she didn't give up, she humbled herself and continued asking. At last, Jesus said, "...your faith is great...," and her daughter was immediately healed.

What was this whole parable about? Was it a question of whether or not it was God's will to heal her daughter? No, it **was** God's will all along. This was a **test** of how great her faith was. This woman, because of her persistence and great faith, brought about God's will for her daughter's life. She must have known enough about God to know that He was a God of love and mercy. Therefore she did not believe it was God's will for her daughter to be sick. So she **continued** asking for Jesus to heal her daughter until she received what she knew **was** God's will.

Most of us would have given up when Jesus did not answer. We would have said, "Well, I guess it was not His will" or, "Well, He did not answer me, so maybe I should forget it." But this woman would not settle for a "no" answer. She never gave up asking. She just kept on asking and asking until she got what she wanted. That is called perseverance!

God wants us to be as persistent as she was and not to give up in order for His will to be accomplished in our lives. If we persevere in prayer and do not give up, we will be effective with God. Mt. 7:7,8 (AMP) says:

Keep on asking and it will be given you; keep on seeking and you will find; keep on knocking (reverently) and the door will be opened to you. For every one who keeps on asking receives and he who keeps on seeking finds and to him who keeps on knocking it will be opened.

In other words, if someone were outside your door, and you were at home but you were ignoring their knocking, after a while if they just continued knocking and knocking, eventually you would get tired of hearing the knocking and go to the door and answer it. In the same way, if your child is hungry and asked you for something to eat, but you ignored him, eventually, if he just kept on asking and asking, you would give in and get him something to eat.

23

I want to share an example of perseverance in prayer in our life—an example of not giving up, and, because of that, bringing God's will about in our daughter's life.

Our daughter, Jennifer, was always a very strong-willed child, but when she turned twelve years old she became very rebellious. It seemed as though the more we spanked her the more rebellious she became! We tried everything you can imagine to discipline her, but to no avail. As she grew older it only got worse and worse until by the time she was sixteen years old, we could not control her at all! You see, God had a wonderful plan for her life, but the devil wanted to completely destroy her, and not only her, but **us** along with her.

We went through what seemed like hell on earth with her. In the natural it looked hopeless, but the love of God compelled us to never give up on her. We knew God had a special call on her life and we prayed and prayed for her. We held onto the prophecies that had been spoken over her life when she was nine years old. Not only that, but we held onto all the promises in God's word for the children of the godly. We continually confessed the word about her and stood on that word. We reminded God of His promise to bless our children.

Many times we fasted and prayed for a week at a time. Finally, we got so mad at the devil that we started yelling at him and demanding him to leave her alone! We would say to him, "Satan, you will never have Jennifer's life. She will never serve you. She will serve Almighty God. She will love God with all of her heart, all of her soul, and all of her mind. She will hate you and all your works.

God will turn for the good everything you have done in her life to destroy her, and He will use it to destroy your kingdom!"

We would always remind satan of this and bind all his evil spirits that we knew were working in her life to destroy her. Because Jennifer was an heir of salvation, according to Hebrews 1:14, we had the authority to commission the ministering spirits of God to go and to minister to her.

We never gave up on her no matter what we saw with our natural eyes. We stood in faith and in **love** and confessed the Word of God over her life. But it was not until we became extremely mad at the devil that we finally began to get the victory!

I wish I could say that after one time of shouting for the victory we won the battle, but it did not happen that way. It took weeks and perhaps even months (I cannot remember exactly how long) for us to win the final battle. But we did get the Victory! God not only brought her to brokenness with godly sorrow that led to repentance, but He **completely** restored her. He has redeemed everything the devil tried to do in her life. She is now a radiant example of God's love and mercy. She truly loves the Lord with all her heart, all her soul, and all her mind!

The Lord is using Jennifer mightily with other young people to bring about restoration to their lives. Glory to God! When she shares with others about what God has done in her life, she says that she learned the mercy and love of God through her parent's unconditional love for her even when she was at her worst.

She understands the power of prayer and perseverance because she learned it by example. She also knows how cunning and deceitful satan is and she realizes that he wanted to destroy her. She hates satan and she teaches others about his lies and schemes and helps them get out of the traps satan has set for their lives. She is very strong in the areas that were her weak points because of our wonderful Redeemer! How I thank Him that he gave us the grace to never give up on her. It took much perseverance and refusing to give up in order to be effective in our prayers for her.

If we persevere in prayer and do not give up, we **will be effective!**

James 5:16 (KJV) says:

*Confess your faults to one another, pray one for another that ye may be healed. **The effectual fervent prayer of a righteous man availeth much!***

Remember, our prayers must become fervent in some cases. The word fervent means "to glow, boil, or rage" or otherwise to get **hot** and **fiery**. We need to get hot and fiery and raging mad when the enemy attempts to defeat us, discourage us, stop us and wipe us out! Too often we just sit back and put up with it. Who can fight a battle with a passive attitude? Would you just sit there and watch as someone broke into your house and stole all your things? Of course not! Can you be passive towards an enemy who comes to kill, steal and destroy? Sometimes we have to get good and mad at the devil to get the victory.

Some of us have a high harassment threshold and we let the enemy push us around, bluff us, walk all over us, until we finally get mad and call upon God saying, "I have had enough, God! What are you going to do about it? Are you not going to help me?"

God answers back, "I have already helped you. I have given **you** all power and authority over the works of the enemy! What are **you** going to do?" Faith without works is dead! We must have not only faith, but our faith has to have action behind it in order to have active faith. Faith without actions is dead faith!

Parents, do you remember the times you have told your children to do something two or three times and they have not listened? Finally, when you have had enough, you get stirred up and you get **LOUD** because now you mean business! Suddenly they began to listen and obey. Well, the devil is, in many ways, like a stubborn, rebellious child. He does not listen and obey unless he knows there is force behind our voice and we are in control of the situation and have taken authority over him.

The kingdom of heaven suffers violence, but the violent take it by force! We must be violent in our faith and persevere in order to bring about, by force, the will of God.

It is written in the Word of God that the gates of hell shall not prevail against the church. Gates stand for power. The powers of hell shall not be able to stand up against the church! The church should be the one on the OFFENSIVE, not the defensive. We are supposed to be knocking the gates of hell down. It is time that the body of Christ rise up and go forth to possess the land. We should be the ones taking the kingdom by force from satan.

It often takes a spiritual battle to obtain victory in the Kingdom of God against the powers of darkness. Spiritual warfare requires us to put on the **whole** armor of God—to take up our weapons and fight.

In 2 Cor. 10:3-4 (KJV) we are told:

*For though we walk in the flesh, we do not war after the flesh. For the weapons of our warfare are not carnal but **mighty** through God to the pulling down of strongholds.*

Prayer and perseverance are so important! That is why we are commanded so many times in the Word of God to pray. We can look at the life of Jesus and see that continually He got alone with His Father in order to pray. Before miracles, and before major decisions, Jesus prayed, sometimes all night long.

Jesus told an important parable about prayer as instruction to us. He said,

Men ought always pray and not to turn coward— faint, lose heart and give up. (Luke 18:1b, AMP)

If we faint, lose heart or give up it means we are not praying enough. Jesus went on to tell a parable to illustrate what He meant by not giving up. Let us read it:

Now He was telling them a parable to show that at all times they ought to pray and not lose heart, saying, "There was in a certain city a judge who did not fear God, and did not respect man. And there was a widow in that city, and she kept coming to him, saying, 'Give me legal protection from my opponent.' And for a while he was unwilling; but afterward he said to himself, 'Even though I do not fear God nor respect man, yet because this widow bothers me, I will give her legal protection, lest by continually coming she wear me out.'" And the Lord said, "Hear what the unrighteous judge said; now shall not God bring about justice for His elect, who cry to Him day and night, and will He delay long over them? I tell you that He will bring about justice for them speedily. However, when the Son of man comes, will He find faith on the earth?" (Luke 18:1-8, NAS)

Here we see the widow kept coming and asking. She never gave up day and night until she received what she wanted. God was saying, "If the unrighteous judge gave her what she wanted because of her persistence, won't I, the Righteous Judge give you what you want because of your persistence and faith?" God was telling us here that we should always pray, and never give up praying, and never give up our faith.

Ephesians 6:18 (AMP) says:

Pray at all times—on every occasion, in every season—in the Spirit, with all manner of prayer and entreaty. To that end keep alert and watch with strong purpose and perseverance, interceding in behalf of all the saints (God's consecrated people).

As children of God, we should pray and persevere until we know that God's will is done in our lives, our families' lives, our neighbors' lives and even within our nation and other nations. God's will is that His kingdom will come on earth as it is in heaven.

Let us not give up and grow weary! Let us not faint and quit! Let us continue to fight until we have overcome and have obtained the victory! **WE CAN TAKE THE KINGDOM OF GOD BY FORCE!**

III

The Shout of Victory!

There is a spiritual weapon that has been missed by the church for centuries which God is beginning to restore. His children are again learning how to use this weapon against demonic powers to bring down strongholds. The weapon is the "shout of victory." As a child of God in these last days, we must understand the importance of this weapon and use it. This weapon confuses the enemy...he runs from this weapon! When the Body of Christ, His Army, begins fighting with this spiritual weapon we will see **great** victories. We must learn to shout **the shout of victory!**

The definition of SHOUT is: "A loud cry, any sudden loud outburst or uproar." A "shout" means "to overwhelm by loud shoutings."[1]

In Hebrew, the word for the verb "shout" is **ruwa** which means to "split the ears with sound; that is, to shout (for alarm or joy); to make a joyful noise." The noun

---

1. *Webster's Dictionary*

form is **teruwah** which means "clamor, that is acclamation of joy, or a battle cry." To shout down is to silence or overwhelm by loud shouting; to shout louder than your opponent.

When a battle is in progress, it is time to start shouting! It is true that the Bible says that satan comes "**as** a roaring lion", but it is also written in Joel 3:16a (KJV):

The lord also shall roar out of Zion and utter His voice from Jerusalem.

Zion, which is the Body of Christ, shall roar in triumphant victory! Notice, satan comes **as** a roaring lion. He really is not a lion at all. But Jesus **is** "the Lion of the Tribe of Judah". We are to overwhelm satan and overcome him. The Church is the only one who will prevail against the gates of hell. We shall prevail and overcome by a loud roar from Zion! Just as the walls of Jericho came falling down, the roar from Zion will cause the gates of hell to fall, and the Church will go in and divide the spoil.

*Let the **high praises** of God be in their mouth, and a two-edged sword in their hand, to execute vengeance on the nations, and punishments on the peoples; to bind their kings with chains, and their nobles with fetters of iron; To execute on them the judgment—this honor have all His saints.* (Ps. 149:6-9, NKJV)

All of God's saints have the **honor** of subduing kingdoms of the enemy; of overcoming his evil works; of binding their kings with chains; of letting the oppressed go free; and of proclaiming the acceptable year of the Lord and the day of vengeance of our God. The devil as the "god of this world" has triumphed long enough! It is time for the Body of Christ to get stirred up with righteous indignation and begin to go in and possess the land which belongs to God in the first place!

There is **power** in shouting. Do not let anyone tell you that you should say only quiet prayers or always keep quiet in church. There is nothing quiet about shouting! Yes, there is absolutely nothing dignified about shouting, but nothing will stop even some of the most dignified people from shouting their home team to a victory at a baseball or football game! And, I ask you, how many Americans do you think sat passively by as they watched the Americans beat the Russians in hockey at the 1980 Olympics to win the gold medal!

Shouting is also used in competitive games as a method of disorienting the opponents. For instance, at basketball games or football games, when the opponent is getting ready to score, we start shouting really loud, not to help them, but to throw them off the mark. Loud shouting disorients and confuses our opponents.

There are times when we have been in trials or times of discouragement and we do not feel like praising God; we do not feel like praying or clapping our hands, but that is the very time God would say to us, "Praise Me. Trust Me. I want you to come into my gates with thanksgiving and with praise. I want you to make a joyful noise—even a sacrifice of praise, the fruit of your lips. I want you to cast your cares upon Me. I want you to rejoice before Me, for the battle is not yours, but it is Mine. I will show Myself mighty on your behalf when you begin praising and worshiping Me."

Carnal weapons are not effective in spiritual warfare. It is imperative that we use the spiritual weapons God has instructed us to use. In the book of Joshua, it is recorded how Joshua, after entering the promised land, received instructions from God on how to conquer the strong-walled city of Jericho. Jericho was the fortress city by which all must pass to enter Canaan. Because the people of Jericho had heard of how mightily and power-fully God had acted on behalf of the Israelites (Joshua 2:10,11), they were terrified and had shut up the entire city so that "none went out and none went in," and for forty years they lived in fear of an Israelite invasion. Con-tinuing on in Joshua 6, God points out to Joshua how He had given Jericho into his hands, but does not call the Is-raelites to battle.

> *Then the Lord said to Joshua, "See, I have delivered Jericho into your hands, along with its king and its fighting men. March around the city once with all the armed men. Do this for six days. Have seven priests carry trumpets of rams' horns in front of the ark. On the seventh day, march around the city seven times, with the priests blowing the trumpets. When you hear them sound a long blast on the trumpets, have all the people give a loud shout; then the wall of the city will collapse and the people will go up, every man straight in."* (Josh. 6:2-5, NIV)

I am certain that at first Joshua could not see the logic of God's plan. However, he did not rely on his own understanding, but he relied on God's faithfulness to keep His word. When Joshua stepped out in faith, he knew it would work. Joshua and the people believed that God was the Most High God, possessor of heaven and earth, and that nothing was impossible with God on their side. Surely He would deliver them from their enemies!

The plan was to march around the city seven days in silence, which they did, and on the seventh day they marched around it seven times. But this seventh day was not a day of silence! God had commanded them to get loud and to shout for the victory as they marched the seventh time, and as they shouted with a **GREAT SHOUT**, the walls came crashing down!

When the trumpets sounded, the people shouted, and at the sound of the trumpet, when the people gave a loud shout, the wall collapsed; so every man charged straight in, and they took the city. (Josh. 6:20, NIV)

Joshua had to obey God in order to have victory over his enemy. In the natural it looked impossible. The walls of Jericho were wide enough for chariots and horses to be driven on top of them. They were made of brick and mortar. There was no possible way in the natural to make the walls fall down. But when Joshua obeyed God's instructions, God himself caused the walls to fall down flat in response to their shouts. You can still go to Jericho today and see the remains of that great wall utterly destroyed.

Joshua and his men made no effort to scale the wall. No weapons were used, nor were other ordinary means of warfare used in any way. The sight of Joshua and his men marching around the walls day after day must have been a merrymaking spectacle to the inhabitants of Jericho. They had never seen or heard of such a seemingly foolish thing. Neither had the Israelites, but they were in strict obedience to the God who uses the foolish things to confound the wise and the weak things to destroy the mighty. (1 Cor. 1:18-31)

In the natural, it may seem foolish to shout for the victory or to rejoice before the answer, but God's ways are not the same as man's ways. His thoughts are not the same as man's thoughts. No, they are much higher and much greater than ours! But when we do things according to God's pattern we will see the enemy defeated!

When your enemy hears you shout thanks to God for the victory **before** the battle is won, it will cause panic and confusion in his camp. When God's Army begins using this weapon, they will see great spiritual strongholds come falling down.

The key to victory is in doing things God's way! It was not because of the children of Israel's strength that the battle was won, but it was in **relying** on the Lord with all their hearts and leaning not to their own understanding. Their faith and trust were in God and when they did and said what He ordered, God gave the miracle of deliverance. It is the same way today: when we trust in God and fight the spiritual battles His way, He will give

us the victory every time. It is important that we persevere and do not give up. For all the promises of God are
obtained through faith and **patience**.

> *Cast not away therefore your confidence which hath
> great recompence of reward. For ye have need of
> **patience**, that, after ye have done the will of God,
> ye might receive the promise.* (Heb. 10:35-36, KJV)

> *That ye be not slothful, but followers of them who
> through **faith** and **patience** inherit the promises.*
> (Heb. 6:12, KJV)

Faith believes **before** it sees the answer. Joshua and
his people could have said on the fifth or sixth day, "Well,
this seems ridiculous, nothing is happening. Let's just forget it!" But they did not quit, they obeyed God to the end.
Never give up until you have won the battle. Faith does
not give up; faith **continues** until it obtains the promise.

We are told that without faith it is impossible to please
God. (Heb. 11:6) And that whatsoever is not of faith is sin.
(Rom. 14:23) We know that, if we are Christians, then we
are the "just" and it is written that "the just shall live by
faith." (Heb. 10:38, KJV) Genuine faith is free from fear.
Genuine faith is thanking God for something you can't
see and is free from any doubt.

When fighting spiritual battles, it does not matter how
small and insignificant or how weak and fearful we may
feel in the natural. What does matter is our faith in a supernatural God who has not changed. He is still able to
perform miracles of deliverance. Our faith must not be in

37

ourselves or even in our faith, but our faith must be in the unchanging character of God. The God who loves us and cares about everything that is happening to us has promised that He will **never, never** leave or forsake us. We must believe that He really is **for** us and that He really wants us to win. Not only that, but because of His great love for us, He will make us more than conquerors through Jesus Christ.

Gideon is an example of a man who believed in the character of God when he asked in Judges 6:13a, (NAS):

Oh, my Lord, if the Lord be with us, why then is all this befallen us? and where be all His miracles which our fathers told us about...

Gideon was hiding from the Midianites. He was fearful. He did not really believe that God was with him. He had not seen any miracles and he could not understand why God had allowed his children to be so oppressed if He really was with them. So he was questioning God. Nevertheless, Gideon chose to start believing God. Because of Gideon's faith, God was able to take this young man and use him to bring deliverance to Israel. Gideon was obedient to the direction of the Lord and fought the battle God's way.

Gideon did not take large numbers of men with weapons of swords with him to fight the battle. God had told him to send away everyone who was fearful and afraid. Thirty-two thousand men were sent home, and Gideon was left with a mere three hundred men to fight the vast armies of the Midianites.

So often God uses us in our weakest areas so that He receives **all** the glory and so that we are not able to glory in ourselves. Gideon knew if God didn't intervene on his behalf that he would surely be defeated. Gideon would never be able to say, "my own power has delivered me." But the angel of the Lord had appeared to him and said to him;

The Lord is with you, O valiant warrior. (Joshua 6:12, NAS)

God saw Gideon as a valiant warrior not as he was, hiding in fear of the enemy. God sees the end from the beginning and calls those things that are not as though they are. (Rom. 4:17) Gideon **chose** to believe that God was with him. He **chose** to believe that if God called him a valiant warrior, then he was. Gideon believed that by faith, God had already given him the victory in the spiritual realm.

We can choose to believe God and not to doubt. We can set our will against doubt just as we do against any other sin; and, as we stand firm and refuse to doubt, but believe God's word, the Holy Spirit will come to our aid and give us the faith of God and crown us with victory.

Gideon took his three hundred men and went to the battle. He divided the three hundred into three groups, and gave every man a trumpet and a clay jar with a torch in it. He told each group to surround the great multitude and as soon as he and his men arrived at their positions, they should blow their trumpets and **SHOUT:**

The sword of the Lord and of Gideon (Judg. 7:20b, KJV)!

They were told to do the same thing in Judges 7:20-22 (LB):

Suddenly they blew their trumpets and broke their clay jars so that their torches blazed into the night. The other two hundred of his men did the same, blowing the trumpets in their right hands, and holding the flaming torches in their left hands all **yelling,** *"for the Lord and for Gideon." Then they just stood and watched as the whole vast army began rushing around in a panic, shouting and running away. For in the confusion the Lord caused the enemy troops to begin fighting and killing each other from one end of the camp to the other, and they fled into the night to places as far away as Beth-shittah near Tererah, and to the border of Abel-meholah near Tabboth.*

There was a great battle won that day, and all of God's children saw the great power of their God. They had conquered their strong enemy without having to fight with natural weapons of warfare. They obeyed God and won the battle.

God tells us to:

Shout with the voice like a trumpet. (Isa. 58:1, KJV)

We have tongues; we need to use them for God's purposes and not the devil's. Let our mouths be like trumpets for God. We are the light of the world. We need to let our light shine brightly for God's glory. We need to be obedient to God and offer Him the sacrifices of our praises—the fruit of our lips.

Gideon's obedience to God's way of fighting and his faith in God's faithful character were very important to obtaining the victory.

The shout of victory is a spiritual weapon. When your enemy hears you thanking God for the victory **before** the battle is won, it will cause him panic and confusion. When God's army begins using this weapon, they will see great spiritual strongholds come falling down!

IV

The Shout Restored

When God first began speaking to me about the "shout of victory," I did not understand exactly what He meant. He had been speaking the word "shout" to me for weeks. I wondered what He might be trying to say, but I made the mistake of not studying the scriptures to try and find out what the Lord might be telling me.

This occurred during a time when God had moved our family to Wisconsin. We were going to be there for two years. I felt that my main purpose for being there was to fast and pray for the Body of Christ, as well as for the lost. I also knew God wanted me to do spiritual warfare for the city. There was a lot of oppression in this city and the Lord identified the powers and principalities that needed to be pulled down in the spiritual realm.

We were just beginning to see victories, when within a week's time our whole family came under satanic attack. We had lived in divine health through faith for many years. However, this attack was violent and fierce!

All four members of our family came down with serious symptoms of different illnesses within a two-week period. My husband was diagnosed as having a kidney problem; our oldest daughter was diagnosed with a problem in her blood. We were told it would take her at least six months to recover and that we would have to take her out of school, because she would have to sleep about twenty hours a day! Our younger daughter's hair started falling out and leaving small round bald spots on her scalp, also the bottom of her feet started peeling. About the same time I read an article telling of a systemic disease which attacked children her age and the disease had these same symptoms! Meanwhile, something happened to my back, and it felt as though I had ruptured a disk. (Having previously had a ruptured disk, I was well aware of how it felt!)

As I was crying out to God for deliverance, the only thing He continued to speak to me was the word, "SHOUT!" Finally, I got my concordance out and began to do a study on shouting as I lay flat on my back in bed. When I read and studied all the scriptures on shouting, God gave me understanding as the Holy Spirit taught me and gave me revelation and insights. I began to realize that shouting was a mighty spiritual weapon.

That evening when my husband, Fred, returned home, I shared the scriptures with him. Fred gathered the family together and read aloud the scriptures on healing and he also read all of Isaiah 53. Then he said, "We are going to shout!"

I asked, "What are we going to shout?" "Just follow me", he replied. At first our daughters felt embarrassed and began laughing, but as they watched, they realized we were serious. Before long they began shouting high praises to God right along with us. We marched through every room in our house shouting "PRAISE THE LORD, HIS MERCIES ENDURE FOREVER, HALLELUJAH, HOSANNA TO THE KING OF KINGS AND THE LORD OF LORDS, GLORY TO GOD FOREVER! BY HIS STRIPES WE ARE HEALED, HALLELUJAH!" By the time we got to the last room in our house, we all looked at each other and started laughing with the joy of the Lord!

Many times the Word says, **"shout for joy"**. That is just what happened to us! We were **filled** with joy! As we ended the evening filled with the joy of the Lord, we felt strengthened and confident that the battle was God's and not ours! The symptoms did not leave that night, but all fear and doubt left, and God's wonderful peace that surpasses **all** understanding guarded our hearts and minds that night. When we awoke the next morning, all four of us had been delivered from the lying symptoms and were perfectly healed! Glory to God! That was our first experience seeing the power of "shouting" high praises to the Lord.

God tells us:

*But let all those that put their trust in Thee rejoice: let them ever **shout** for joy, because **thou** defendest them: let them also that love thy name be joyful in thee* (Ps. 5:11, KJV).

Be glad in the LORD and rejoice ye righteous and **shout** *for joy all ye that are upright in heart* (Ps. 32:11, KJV).

Shout *joyfully to the Lord, all the earth. Serve the Lord with gladness; come before Him with joyful singing* (Ps. 100:1, NAS).

Shout *joyfully to God, all the earth; sing the glory of His name; make His praise glorious* (Ps. 66:1, NAS).

The above scriptures establish the fact that God has indeed commanded us to shout for joy to the Lord. When you are discouraged, it is time to start shouting, because shouting brings joy. That is why we are told to shout **for** joy. Notice how many times the scriptures talk about "shouting for joy." Joy is an important fruit of the Spirit, because we are told that the joy of the Lord **is** our **strength** (Neh. 8:10c).

The Hebrew word here for "strength" is "mew-oze" meaning "a defense or fortress, or force." So we could say it this way; the joy of the Lord is our defense. Strength also means energy or force inside us. The joy God gives us when we shout and praise Him is a spiritual energy or strength that brings us the ability to stand in faith and "having done **all** to stand."

If the devil cannot rob you of your joy, he will not be able to defeat you! But if you allow negative thoughts and circumstances to fill your mind instead of God's Word, you will get into discouragement, despair, grief, sorrow, and even self-pity, which the devil loves! He can easily conquer that kind of a Christian. When you have discouragement and no joy you become defenseless to the attacks of the enemy. God instructs us to **guard** our hearts and minds with all **diligence**, for from them flow the issues of **life**.

Let's look at Proverbs 4:20-23 (AMP):

*My son, attend to my words; consent and submit to my sayings. Let them **not depart** from your sight, keep them in the center of your heart. For they are **life** to those who find them, healing and health to all their flesh. Keep your heart with all diligence and above all that you guard, for out of it flow the springs of life.*

Here, God is very serious bout our "guarding" or "watching over" our hearts or thoughts. He also tells us that we are to be "transformed by the **renewing** of our minds" (Rom. 12:1,2). In Phillipians 4 we are told to **think** on things above, not on the earth. We are told to only think about those things which are lovely, good, true, pure, excellent, and of good report. **Our thoughts are so important, because as a man thinketh in his heart so is he.** (Prov. 23:7a). In other words, what you **think** about, you will eventually believe and act out.

Satan brings "fiery darts" or lying thoughts. We are told to put up our "shield of faith" to quench **all** his fiery darts. If we have our shield of faith up, when the fiery darts come we will not agree with anything that does not line up with the Word of God. We must obey the Word of

God in order to be fruitful and enjoy life. Joy is one of the fruits of obedience to God's Word. Joy is to be a **defense** against the enemy.

As you shout praises to God and sing praises to Him you will find that joy comes to you! So we can shout to have joy if we lack it. Try putting this principle into practice the next time you feel a lack of joy. Take five minutes to shout praises to God and you will see your joy return. Joy is also a **choice** or a **decision** we make.

God says to;

Rejoice always and pray without ceasing, in everything give thanks; for this is God's will for you in Christ Jesus (1 Thess. 5:16-18, NAS).

We are even told to offer a sacrifice of praise to God continually, that is, the fruit of our lips giving thanks to His Name.

When we do not feel like praising God, that is when we have the opportunity to offer a sacrifice of praise to God. We cannot respond to our feelings. We have to respond to God's Word and obey it in order to have success. Carnal Christians act on their feelings rather than putting God's Word **first**. Their feelings control their thoughts and their actions. They live defeated Christian lives because of their disobedience. Feelings are subject to change daily, but God's Word will never change!

There are over sixty scriptures that command us to rejoice, such as the following:

Be glad in the Lord and rejoice you righteous ones, and shout for joy all you who are upright in heart. (Ps. 32:11, NAS)

The Lord reigns; let the earth rejoice; let the multitudes of isles and coastlands be glad! (Ps. 97:1, AMP)

The word rejoice here is of any violent emotion, i.e. usually rejoice or exceedingly glad. Do you see rejoicing upon the earth? Psalms 97 indicates that the very earth spins because of rejoicing in its Creator! Do you realize that you as a child of God can rejoice during times of trouble and discouragement? It is a matter of making a **decision** to rejoice and to be glad regardless of how you feel. Simply because you want to please and obey God.

The Hebrew word for rejoice is "alza" which means to exalt because of victory. We are told to be exceedingly glad—this is a **decision** of the will. Once we **decide** to rejoice there will be more power and strength in our daily lives. We are even told:

A merry heart doeth good like a medicine. But a broken spirit drieth the bones (Prov. 17:22, KJV).

A merry heart is a healthful heart, but anyone completely broken in spirit and dejected can develop many bodily illnesses. Nothing ruins health more than grief, continual worry, anxiety, discouragement, fretfulness, bad tempers, hatred and malice. The end of these things is spiritual destruction and possibly even death. We should rid ourselves of such health-destroying agencies.

These things are part of the old self which we are told to put off. We must put on the new man (which is Jesus) if we want to obey God and have success. Jesus is not depressed and defeated. His spirit is living on the inside of us, but we must yield to His spirit and ignore the "feelings" of the flesh.

Ezra told God's people:

Be not grieved and depressed, for the joy of the Lord is your strength and stronghold (Neh. 8:10, AMP).

If the devil cannot steal your joy, he will never be able to defeat you, and he will not be able to rob you of your strength! That is why God tells us to **rejoice always**. Yes, to even count it **joy** when we go through trials. It is when we are in the midst of those trials that we really need to begin praising and thanking God and rejoicing in His ability to deliver us! That shows God that we have faith in Him, and it is very pleasing to Him. It shows the devil that our confidence is in God and that we are not going to let the circumstances control our emotions and thoughts.

There have been times at our church when we have felt oppression in the atmosphere, and after five or ten minutes of everyone shouting high praises to God, the oppression leaves and a joy comes in its place. The Word tells us that He gives us the "garment of praise for the spirit of heaviness" (Is. 61:3). We must put on the garment of praise whenever we sense that evil spirit of heaviness around. You will see the devil flee, as I have, every time. And do not stop your praises until you know that the heaviness is gone. God inhabits the praises of His people. When Almighty God comes on the scene you had better believe that the enemy flees!!

God is truly restoring to His church the "Shout of Praise." Let us rejoice and be glad for His goodness!

At the same time that the Lord is restoring the shout to the Church, the devil is also using his counterfeit. On Feb. 1, 1990 I read an article in our local newspaper, the "Vienna Times" which reported a "possible occult link to Herndon grave vandalism." One of the items the police recovered from the car of satan worshipers was a cassette tape by the music group "Motley Crue;" the title of the tape was **"Shout at the Devil."**

I since have been told that the song *Shout at the Devil* is a satanic call to arms for the youth of America. While God is restoring the Shout to the church, His enemy is also using the shout for the kingdom of darkness. With every principle of God, satan uses his counterfeit. The Church must **wake up** and realize that the devil means business.

Let us attack the devil's kingdom with the "shout of victory". Let the body of Christ rise up with our mighty offensive weapon of shouting praises to our God! Let the SHOUT BE RESTORED TO THE CHURCH as we go forth to possess the land for our God!

V

The War Cry

*Let the wilderness and its cities lift up their voices, the settlements where Kedar inhabits. Let the inhabitants of Sela sing aloud, let them **shout** for joy from the tops of the mountains. Let them give glory to the Lord, and declare His praise in the coast lands. The Lord will go forth like a warrior, He will arouse His zeal like a man of war. He will utter a shout, yes, He will raise a **WAR CRY**. He will prevail against His enemies. I have kept silent for a long time, I have kept still and restrained Myself: Now like a woman in labor, I will groan, I will gasp and pant. (Is. 42:11-14, NAS)*

Here we see that the LORD will raise a **WAR CRY**. And that He will prevail against His enemies. In other words, He will cry out the "war cry" and come against His enemies. How will this happen? Through His Word, but also through His people. For He has said, "You shall be my mouthpiece" (Jer. 1). It is through the body of Christ that the war cry will be raised. We are told here that the Lord shall go forth as a mighty man—like a man of war!

The Lord is beginning to pour out on the body of Christ a mighty warring spirit—an overcoming spirit instead of a cowardly spirit. As we come closer to the second coming of Jesus, our "Victorious Warrior," I believe we will see God's people become very strong and courageous. When we see injustice being done by the evil one, we will put our foot down and demand in the mighty name of JESUS that the enemy flee!

Many times in the Old Testament we see God's children overcoming their enemy by **shouting high praises to God**, and by using the war cry in battle. Let us look at the story of David and the giant, a young shepherd boy, had come to watch his brothers fight against Goliath.

> *So David rose early in the morning and left the flock with a keeper and took the supplies and went as Jesse had commanded him. And he came to the circle of the camp while the army was going out in battle array **shouting the war cry**.* (Sam. 17:20, NAS)

Everyone, except David, was afraid of the giant. David knew how absurd it was to be intimidated by this heathen Philistine whose power was nothing next to God's power. David proclaimed in verse 26:

> *For who is this uncircumcised Philistine, that he should defy the armies of the living God?*

David knew that he was in a covenant with God. He understood that God would cause his enemies to flee in seven directions and that he (David) was the head and not the tail, and that with God on his side, no matter how powerful the giant was, he would conquer because God was greater. David knew that Jehovah the Almighty was behind his actions, therefore, nothing was too hard or too impossible for him. So David went up to the battle with a **shout** and confessed with his mouth what he knew in his heart—that God would deliver the giant into his hands.

After David had defeated the giant, the men of Israel arose and **shouted** and pursued the Philistines and defeated them. Here we see two incidents of shouting before the battle was won. These examples have been recorded so that we might learn God's principles and see how effective shouting is as a weapon.

In II Chronicles, there is an account of how shouting caused the enemy to be disoriented and confused and of how they even began fighting each other. Here we see a battle between Judah and Israel:

*When Judah turned around, behold, they were at-tacked both front and rear; so they cried to the Lord, and the priests blew the trumpets. Then the men of Judah raised the **war cry**, and when the men of Judah raised a war cry, then it was that God routed Jeroboam and all Israel before Abijah and Judah. And when the sons of Israel fled before Judah, God gave them into their hand. And Abijah and his people defeated them with a great slaughter, so that 500,000 chosen men of Israel fell slain. Thus the sons of Israel were subdued at that time, and the* *sons of Judah conquered because they trusted in the Lord, the God of their fathers.* (2 Chr. 13:14-18, NAS)

Notice that the passage shows that God smote their enemy as they raised the war cry. It is as we are shouting our high praises to God that God is moving on our behalf against the enemy.

As we learn more and more about warfare and receive more revelation of the power of God and of the will of God, we will get indignant when we see the enemy's devices.

The strategy of satan has been to cause us to get our eyes off God and His greatness, to take our eyes off His promises and His word and onto the people, problems or circumstances when we are in the midst of trials. The father of lies has deceived us into believing that we are indeed fighting against "human flesh" instead of his evil powers and principalities.

This deception has caused us to fight one another instead of turning our anger against the real culprit! Satan wants the Body of Christ to be ignorant of his evil devices so he can continue to cause division, jealousy, fear, and hatred among God's people. He knows that if we ever got into love and unity with each other, and we really believed the Bible was true about our victory through Christ, we would completely destroy his works.

For centuries the "accuser of the brethren" has worked in and through God's people to bring accusations against each other instead of against him. God's word has told us that when the Body of Christ love one another, and are in **unity**, the whole world would know that God sent Jesus.

Neither for these alone do I pray—it is not for their sake only that I make this request—but also for all those who will ever come to believe in (trust, cling to, rely on) Me through their word and teaching; So that they all may be one (just) as You, Father, are in Me and I in You, that they also may be one in Us, so that the world may believe and be convinced that You have sent Me. (John 17:20-21, AMP)

The strategy of the devil is **always** to divide and to conquer. If he can divide us, then he will win the battle. This tactic has been used by the devil for ages. He uses it on families, friends, prayer groups, churches, etc. He uses irritations, pride, jealousy, insecurity, misunderstandings, and anything else he can possibly use to cause us to criticize and to judge one another. He puts thoughts into our minds of how neglected we are, or of how we have been wronged by the other person. Satan is always trying to get us into self-pity, fear, anger and division.

God tells us to **FORGET** about ourselves and to keep our minds on Him; to not think about what others can do for us but what we can do for others. We get so self-centered that we fail to understand how we can meet the other person's needs and be a blessing to them. So we fall into satan's trap and instead of laying our life down and counting the other as better than ourselves, we end up doing just the opposite! Strife and division get in, and then we lose many battles.

We need to become aware of how we fall into the enemy's snares and traps, and start out-smarting him for a change. The secret is just so simple and, yet, so difficult sometimes. And that is to humble ourselves and to obey the Word of God, which teaches us to really love and to forgive one another from our heart.

When the whole Body of Christ gets into unity and love, there will be so much power and so many blessings from God that we will easily defeat the enemy.

*Behold, how good and how pleasant it is for brethren to dwell together in unity! It is like the precious ointment upon the head, that ran down upon the beard, even Aaron's beard: that went down to the skirts of his garments; It as the dew of Hermon, that descended upon the mountains of Zion: for **there the Lord commanded the blessing,** even life for evermore. (Ps. 133, KJV)*

Notice we are told that it is good and pleasant when we are together in unity; it is there the Lord commands His blessings! It is vitally important that we stay in unity. There are many promises of God that have to do with unity and love. But ignorance, fear, unbelief and disobedience to God's word have hindered and destroyed many. We need to have a knowledge of who our enemy is and what his schemes are, but at the same time, we must believe the truth about his defeat. Ask God to give you a Holy Spirit-inspired revelation of the truth about who you are in Christ Jesus and what it means when He says,

"Greater is He that is in you than he that is in the world!" (1 John 4:4)

Many of God's children live far below the level of blessings that God desires for them because they do not believe in or **do** the Word of God. God would have us live the resurrected life, the victorious life, the overcoming life instead of always being defeated. So often we have been deceived into believing that "it must be God's will that I'm defeated, that I'm not overcoming this problem" **NO**, it is not God's will at all! We have just believed too many lies from the father of lies himself!

We **must** believe God's word in spite of all the outward circumstances and start thanking Him for the truth of His Word. We need to say, "Thank you Lord that even though I don't feel like it, I believe that Jesus is on the inside of me and I believe that Greater is Jesus inside me than he who is in the world. Thank you Father that your Word has promised me that you will **always** cause me to overcome through Christ who lives in me! I accept your Word as true regardless of what the outward circumstances tell me. After all, these circumstances are subject to change, but your Word is not subject to change."

"Thank you Father that you will never leave me nor forsake me and that whatever happens you will work everything out for my good and for your glory. Thank you Lord that you will help me be led by your Spirit and not by my flesh. Thank you Father for your mighty powerful Holy Spirit who is on the inside of me leading and guiding me! Praise your holy name for the victory!" Amen!

God's Spirit is on the inside of us, and if we yield to that Spirit and walk in the Spirit and not yield to the flesh, we **will have victory!** The mighty Spirit of God will rise up and flow out of us as rivers of living waters. The Holy Spirit wants to be the one who is our leader and guide, our comforter and our counselor, He wants to be strong inside us and in control of our lives. He wants to praise the Father through our lips and help us even to offer a sacrifice of praise when it's not easy. The Holy Spirit desires to glorify the Father and to bless Jesus Christ through us.

The Holy Spirit is moving throughout the whole Body of Christ today and He is bringing forth many new songs. Songs of warfare, songs of shouting, songs of deliverance, songs of victory! This is the Spirit of Almighty God doing this work. No man could ever do what God is doing! There is an anointing coming forth of new strength and power as never before. One of the reasons for this new power is that many have been brought to their knees in repentance for their sins as God has been purging His body. With this cleansing work, we will see more power than ever before being displayed in the body of Christ. There will be more revelation about how to fight the battles and win. As we receive understanding about how to win the battle, and we become obedient to **do** the Word, the God of our battles **will** fight for us!

In order to engage in the fight we first must recognize and believe that there **is** a real battle taking place in the heavenlies. Then we have to understand how to fight in the battle. Our Commander in Chief has to give us His marching orders for each battle. But we always need to **be prepared** for an attack should we encounter one. One of the ways we can be prepared is to know about the value of the "war cry." I am not saying that I have full understanding yet, but I am pressing in to try to receive more revelation and understanding about the value of the "war cry." Apparently, the children of Israel knew what a "war cry" meant, and they used the "war cry" in battles.

Because Joshua was familiar with the ways in which men prepared for war, when he heard a **shouting** coming from the camp of the Israelites, he exclaimed to Moses, "There is a noise of war in the camp". (Exodus 32:17, KJV) It was a custom for men to be shouting the war cry before the battle. So when Joshua heard the loud noise, he thought the men were preparing for war.

If you study the history of wars between nations, you will find that the kings had the "call to arms" sounded, or the "war cry." This sound signaled the warriors to attack their enemy. We see an account of this in 1 Samuel 17:20 (NAS):

*So David arose early in the morning and left the flock with a keeper and took the supplies and went as Jesse had commanded him. And he came to the circle of the camp while the army was going out in battle array **shouting the war cry.***

To be "at war" means an active hostile conflict, contention, struggle against the enemy. It is a military term meaning, active armed conflict.

The war cry is a loud, piercing cry or wail or shout. Webster's dictionary says it is a "loud vocal sound expressing pain, anger, fright, joy, etc."

The war cry was a familiar term to the children of Israel. They used it to **intimidate** their enemy. In much the same way the early Indians cried the war cry before and during their attack of the cowboys during the early history of our nation.

Throughout history there has been shouting or loud cries before the battle. We have all seen pictures or movies where the Indians attacking settlers or pioneers let out loud whoops in order to increase intimidation during the attack. In karate, just before the person breaks an object with his hand, we always hear him make a loud, abrupt noise.

Also, in competitive sports such as basketball and football, when the opponent is getting ready to score, we start getting loud and shouting. Why? It is not to help the opponents, but to **throw them off the mark!** Loud shouting disorients and confuses our opponents.

During the Korean War, the American forces had driven the North Koreans back all the way to the Red Chinese border. Suddenly, across the border came hundreds of thousands of Red Chinese soldiers in an attack on the Americans. Most of them were yelling and screaming, and within a short time, the enemy forces had secured North Korea again. Many of the American soldiers reported that there was so much noise it tended to make them believe that there were more enemy soldiers than there really were. Thus the noise caused fear, confusion and defeat.

Amos 1:14 (KJV) talks about "shouting in the day of battle." When you are in the midst of a battle, it is time to start shouting. The "shout of victory" is a spiritual weapon. When the enemy hears you thanking God for the victory before the battle is won, it intimidates him, and it throws him into confusion. When God's army begins using this weapon, they will see great spiritual strongholds come falling down. There will not be any walls too high to tear down nor any circumstances too hard to overcome!

The loud piercing war cry will go out into the darkness and pierce through the evil forces and break down barriers! In my spirit it is as if I see thick dark clouds of evil forces in the heavenlies and the loud shrill sound of the war cry piercing a hole through the center, penetrating all the way through to the light. Then all the prayers that are sitting underneath the dark clouds suddenly begin escaping into the hole of light and reaching heaven!

I believe that there are times that we are in such a battle that all our prayers are being hindered by the opposition. But when we get angry and declare war on the enemy and run to the battle instead of away from it, we will see great victories in our life!

We are in a war so we might as well accept that fact and make the decision that we are going to have the victory. We need to put the full armor of God on and fight. We need to learn how to cry out the war cry!

We need to say, "I will not be overcome. I will not lose heart. I will not give up or be defeated! For my God is the greatest and most powerful force on this earth. There is nothing too hard for Him! With Him on my side, how can I fail, for He **always** causes me to triumph through Christ Jesus! Hallelujah!" Now that is something to shout about! Praise the Lord forever!!

We are told;

You are My war-club, My weapon of war; And with you I shatter nations. And with you I destroy kingdoms. (Jer. 51:20, NAS)

We are to be used as God's war club; His weapon of war! He will shatter nations and destroy satanic kingdoms through us!

I have had several experiences in prayer with other intercessors when the Lord has caused us to become so violently angry with the enemy that we cried out with loud war cries. One occasion was at my sister's house. The Lord had revealed to three of us that a spirit of destruction had been assigned to their home. We went into her basement where we could sense the presence of an evil force. The Lord showed us it was a "spirit of destruction." We prayed, did battle, but could not seem to get the victory. We all knew in our spirits that the evil spirit was still in the room. After we did a mighty war cry, we began to feel a difference in the atmosphere! So we prayed more fervently and used the war cry again. This time we all **knew** we had the victory! We spent several hours praying that night before we won the battle, but it was well worth it because the wonderful presence of God came in a magnificent way! As we finished, we all felt refreshed and full of joy, knowing the battle had been won once again!

That has been more than a year ago since we prayed for her home. Before we had prayed, they had been besieged with financial problems and with constant repair bills due to everything breaking down in their home. Since the victory in the spiritual realm, they have **not** been harassed by constant repair bills and financial problems.

We learned that every previous owner of that house had gone bankrupt while living there! However since we shouted for the victory, my sister says the house has not been the same! The presence of the Lord remains there, and many have since been baptized in her backyard pool. Not only that, many have experienced God in supernatural ways in her home. Instead of there being a curse on her home, there is now the blessings of God! Praise the Lord!

I would encourage you to seek the Lord about this in prayer and ask Him for further revelation and understanding of the "war cry." I realize this may be something new to many in the body of Christ, but I truly believe God will give us more revelation of the value of the "war cry" as the battle gets more fierce.

VI

Crying Out!

You may be in more of an intense battle than you realize. If you find it difficult to praise the Lord, if you feel oppressed, downtrodden, depressed, or discouraged, then you **are** in a raging battle. Your battle is not one that you can see with your natural eyes, but it is a spiritual battle. You need to FIGHT it with spiritual weapons. Perhaps it is time to CRY OUT to God for a breakthrough. To "cry out to God" means to make yourself 100% available to God regardless of the time or cost; to fervently seek Him with all of your heart. Crying out to God is a form of shouting. When a person is crying out to God, he is fervently petitioning in a loud voice for his needs or the needs of others.

We see the story in Luke 18:39 (KJV) of the blind beggar who heard that Jesus was passing by the crowd. This man had a real opportunity to be depressed, but he did not want to miss Jesus. The blind man knew that if only Jesus could hear him, he might have mercy and heal him. So he cried out, "Jesus, Son of David, have mercy on me!"

Everyone around rebuked him and told him to be quiet. But the blind man just cried louder and louder, "Jesus, thou son of David have mercy on me." The Amplified Bible says, "Yet he **screamed** and shrieked so much the more, 'Jesus, Son of David, take pity and have mercy on me!'" Over and over he cried until finally he got Jesus' attention. Jesus asked for the man who was **crying out** to be brought to Him. When he came, Jesus asked him what he wanted. When the blind man answered, "Lord, that I may receive my sight," Jesus answered, "Receive thy sight; thy faith hath saved thee." In response to his cries, Jesus met his need. And immediately he received his sight and followed Jesus, glorifying God.

If the blind man had been intimidated by those around him who did not believe that Jesus would have done anything for him, he would have gotten discouraged and given up. But he refused their rejection and kept on crying out to Jesus. Had he given up, he would have never received his sight! Had he listened to those around him and shut up, he would have remained blind!

It is important that we do not let those around us intimidate us by their unbelief. There may be others around us, even our family and friends, who just do not believe in us or do not believe in the greatness of God; those who at times will discourage us by their doubt and unbelief. But we cannot let discouragement cause us to give up. No, we must continue to fervently cry out to God for the answer until we receive the promise!

In 2 Chronicles 15, there is an interesting story of King Asa and all of Judah and Benjamin seeking the Lord with all of their hearts during a time of many battles. When they were in great trouble, they set their faces to seek God; they sought Him with **all** their heart. They got rid of all their idols and cried out to God for help. As they repented and sought God, He met their need.

> *And they entered into a covenant to seek the Lord God of their fathers with all their heart and with all their soul; that whosoever would not seek the Lord God of Israel should be put to death, whether small or great, whether man or woman. And they swore unto the Lord with a loud voice and* ***with shoutings*** *and with trumpets, and with cornets. And all Judah rejoiced at the oath; for they had sworn with all their heart, and sought him with their whole desire; and he was found of them: and* ***the Lord gave them rest round about***. (II Chron. 15:12, KJV)

When the children of Israel made God their priority, got rid of their idols, and sought God intently with all their hearts, they found him, and they had rest from their enemies for thirty-five years! They must have been very serious about seeking God. Can you imagine putting someone to death, even a child, if they would not seek God? But that is exactly what they had told God they would do! Read the above scripture again and think about it. Should we not, as God's children, also be very serious about seeking the Lord? It was because of their seeking God so intently that He was found of them, and He gave them complete victory. We are told that they sought God with **"their whole desire."** That means the **only** thing that they desired to do was to seek Him. God wants us to desire Him more than any other thing or any other person and to put Him first place in everything. That is a very important key to victory. God talks about this key to victory:

Whenever you have thrown away your idols, I have shown you my power. With one word I have saved you. You have seen me do it; you are my witnesses that it is true. From eternity to eternity I am God. No one can oppose what I do. (Isa. 43:12,13, LB)

There is a spiritual principal here: when we get rid of all of the idols in our hearts, and seek God fervently with all of our hearts, we are promised: not only shall we find Him, but He will cause us to triumph over all our enemies. An "idol" is an object of worship or something that you honor or devote yourself to; something upon which you place value and importance.

In America, there are many idols such as money, materialism, television, food, entertainment, and sports. Anything one considers more important than God (including self) is an idol. Even the daily newspaper can be an idol. Some people consider the newspaper more important than God's Word. They spend thirty minutes daily reading the newspaper but only five minutes reading the Word of God. This is putting higher value or importance in the newspaper—television, etc. than in the Word of God. An idol is **anything more important to you than**

God Himself. It can even be a person. But God is a jealous God:

Are we trying to arouse the Lord's jealousy? Are we stronger than He? (1 Cor. 10:22, NIV)

God loves us with a more intense love than a husband has for his wife. Naturally, a husband would be jealous if his wife wanted to spend her time with someone else other than him. In the same way, God is jealous of those things and people we prefer more than Him. He wants us to love Him in the same way that He loves us. He has promised us, if we will "delight ourselves in Him, He will give us the desires of our heart." (Ps. 37:4) Delight means, "to take great pleasure, have joyful satisfaction, extreme pleasure, to love, appreciate and value as very important."[1] If we take extreme pleasure in God and love and appreciate Him, if we value Him above **all else**, God promises to give us the desires of our heart. We **must** get rid of any and all idols in our heart, and put God first in our lives. When we do, God causes us to have victory and to overcome in every area of our life. We are told to seek **first** the kingdom of God and His righteousness. When we seek Him with our whole heart, we **shall** find Him.

As we come into the very presence of God, there is joy; there is healing; there is answered prayer. Hallelujah! In the presence of the Lord, there is fulness of joy. The joy of the Lord is our strength! Being in the presence of the Lord will give you the faith and the courage it takes to

---

1. *Webster's Dictionary*

count it all joy when going through a trial, regardless of the outcome.

In Isa. 43:1,2 (NAS) the Lord says:

But now, thus says the Lord, your Creator, O Jacob, and He who formed you, O Israel, do not fear, for I have redeemed you; I have called you by name; you are mine! When you pass through the waters, I will be with you; And through the rivers, they will not overflow you. When you walk through the fire, you will not be scorched, nor will the flame burn you.

This passage is not saying that He will not allow us to go through the rivers and the fires. The rivers are problems and troubles, and the fires are trials and testings. God does not say we will escape from them, but that when we go through them, He will be with us and that we will not be hurt. In fact, we will not even be "scorched" which means, superficially, burned or **slightly** burned. We will not even be slightly effected by it in a negative way, because God will see to it that **He** is with us, and **He** will get us safely through it. Not only that, but we will become stronger **because** of the trials. That is why we are instructed in James 1:2 (NAS) to:

Consider it all joy when we encounter various trials.

You can have confidence that as you walk through the fire, you will not be burned; for God will preserve you. If you go through the rivers, they shall not overflow you. The Lord God Almighty will be with you, and His divine presence will see you through to the other side victorious-ly! The Lord promises us:

The eyes of the Lord are upon the righteous, and His ears are open unto their CRY. (Ps. 34:15, KJV)

*The righteous CRY, and the Lord heareth, and delivereth them out of **all** their troubles. (Ps. 34:17, KJV)*

Crying and shouting are similar, in that, they both are loud, strong, and both fervently aimed at God, looking for His deliverance and help.

A friend, Aimy, shared with me her testimony of how the Lord delivered her of "Crohn's" disease. Fifteen years earlier the Lord had sovereignly and supernaturally healed her of Crohn's disease. However, the symptoms of the disease had come back. One day as she was trying to get home to her children, she had to stop her car on the side of the road due to intense pain. She sat in the car racked with pain, praying and crying out to God to deliver her of the Crohn's disease that had left her intestines ravaged by the disease.

As she pleaded with God to deliver her from the pain, she sat unable to move as though something had an in-tense grip on her intestines and had cruelly twisted them about.

She cried out in tears; "Please God enable me to make it home to my children who need me!" When she suddenly heard the voice of the Lord speak to her: "You are talking

73

to the wrong person. I have healed you and I want good for you."

All at once she knew what to do! The revelation that God was **for her**, and that it was the **enemy** who was afflicting her, flooded her mind. Her tears of self-pity and sorrow turned into the weapon of warfare to bring down the stronghold that satan had upon her life. She commanded the enemy to get away from her, reminding him that he had absolutely no right to touch her. She asked God to send His angels to assist her in the warfare. As she shouted with raging anger at the devil, the fear of the disease left, and she knew God's power could drive the enemy from her.

Realizing that the devil had been taunting and tormenting her with fear and symptoms of the disease, she thought to herself, "I'm going to put fear into the devil and torment him! He has **no right** to touch me! I belong to Almighty God and He is on my side!" Crying out and shouting praises to God with all her might and strength, she focused on His victory on the cross knowing the enemy would have to flee!

The release came moments later as the clenching grip of pain subsided and peace and joy filled her heart. In awe of God's power and love she cried and thanked God all the way home, knowing full well a **miracle** had just happened! She had gotten the victory over her enemy! Praise the Lord!

Three years have passed since that battle, and she still remains healed to this day. Thank God she had the grace and courage to cry out for help and to defy the devil. At the time she could have very easily given up and accepted the disease. But she didn't give up! She fought the good fight of faith! She proved to herself and her enemy, that God's Spirit that was on the inside of her was **greater** than the powers of satan.

The key to Aimy's victory was that she didn't give up in despair when she was in terrible pain. She kept crying out to God for help. We must understand the importance of not giving up. We must not become discouraged and filled with self-pity. We must continue to cry out to God in times of trouble.

When Jesus was teaching on prayer in Luke 18, he told the parable of the woman and the unjust judge. He was trying to get His disciples to understand the importance of always praying and not fainting, losing heart, turning cowardly, or giving up when He said:

And shall not God avenge His own elect, which **CRY** *day and night unto Him, though He bear long with them? I tell you that He will avenge them speedily.* (Luke 18:7, KJV)

So often I have seen Christians pray a few times and quote a few scriptures, and when nothing happens, they say, "Well, it must not have been God's will." That is called fainting, losing heart, turning cowardly, and giving up! God does not want His children acting like that! Over and over God tells us to fear not, be strong, have courage and do not give up! If you **know** what the will of God is, then you must **stand**, face the battle and go forward. God will take you **through** the fire (not around it), and you will not be burned. He will take you **through** the waters, and they shall not overwhelm you. For He is the Lord your God, mighty in battle; the **Lord of Hosts** is His name. He is not defeated. He never has been, and He never will be. Hallelujah!

Are you facing a serious trial, perhaps even a threatening disease or death? Call upon the Lord who is great and greatly to be praised. When you set the Lord continually before you, you shall not be moved, for He is at your right hand. He is your rock, your fortress and your deliverer. He shall be your strength and shield, your high tower. He has said, "I will never leave you or forsake you, my child, no **never, never** will I leave your side!" He will deliver you because He loves you and cares for you. Rely on Him, put your confidence in His faithfulness, His loving kindness and His mercies which are new every morning. God is on your side; He is not against you! It is the devil who has come to kill, to steal, and to destroy. You must not permit him to go one step further. Bind him, withstand him and begin shouting; for the battle is God's, and God is always victorious!! Have faith in God.

My secretary had been typing this manuscript, and one evening she returned from work to strife in her home. For eight years she and her husband had been struggling in a very stormy marriage situation. While there had been many breakthroughs in their lives, there were some strongholds to be broken down. Standing on God's promised victory, she told her husband a little bit about my book. He looked at her with a questioning look, but offered no comment. She then said that she was "going upstairs to do some shouting" and told the children not to be alarmed by it all. About fifteen minutes after she had been shouting high praises to God, her husband came walking up the stairs shouting praises to God! She stopped shouting and looked with great surprise at her husband. He said, "I don't understand it, but it works! Things are different around here!" The two of them praised God together.

If you trust Him, He **will** be your shield, because Psalm 18:30b (AMP) says,

God is a shield to those who take refuge and put their trust in Him.

So, trust Him, and put your full confidence in God. When the pressures come, cry out to God and see the results! Even when you do not feel like trusting Him, say "Lord, I trust you." Faith calls those things that are not as though they are. Faith pleases God; faith says, "I trust you, God, even though I don't see the answer."

We are told, "He who trusts the Lord will **prosper**, but he who trusts in himself is a fool." (Prov. 28:25,26) And again, "Fear of man will prove to be a snare, but whoever trusts in the Lord is kept safe." (Prov. 29:25, NIV)

It is better to put our trust and confidence in God and in His Word than to trust others or even ourselves. God can be trusted because He never lies; He is full of truth. When in a desperate situation, put your full trust in Almighty God and His ability to help you. Turn to Him and cry out to Him for mercy and help in a time of need.

*They **cried out to the LORD** in their trouble, and he saved them from their distress.* (Ps. 107:19, NIV)

*Then they **cried out to the LORD** in their trouble, and he brought them out of their distress.* (Ps. 107:28, NIV)

*May my **cry** come before you O Lord; give me understanding according to your word.* (Ps. 19:169, NIV)

*I **cry** to you, O Lord; I say, "You are my refuge, my portion in the land of the living." Listen to my **cry** for I am in desperate need; rescue me from those who pursue me, for they are too strong for me.* (Ps. 142:5,6, NIV)

If you were to do a study on crying out to the Lord, you would find that there are over a hundred scriptures that talk about crying out to God. When you are in trouble, when you need God's wisdom, when in a desperate situation, turn your face like flint and seek the Lord. Cry out to Him day and night until He hears and answers your cry for help. Surely He will rescue you and deliver you, for He hears when the just cry out to Him in times of need.

VII

Shout in Triumph

The definition for the word "triumph" is, "the act or fact of being victorious; victory; achievement; exultation or joy over a victory or achievement. In ancient Rome a procession celebrating the return of a victorious general and his army; to celebrate or rejoice over a victory."[1]

We are told by the Lord that He will always cause us to triumph in Christ. And that the battles have already been won; now we are to enter into His rest. Now is the time to shout in triumph over our victory. Of course it takes great faith to **believe** that you have already got the victory **before** you see it. But if we really believe, then we will act like it, otherwise, it would be **dead faith** without any works. Faith without works is dead.

*But are you willing to recognize, you foolish fellow, that **faith without works is useless?*** (James 2:20, NAS)

---

1.   *Webster's Dictionary*

True faith is calling those things that are not as though they are. True faith is active. If we do not have faith plus actions, it will not do us any good. Faith alone is not enough, we must **do** something to make our faith **work** for us. **There has to be a corresponding action.** If we really believe, then we will be rejoicing instead of fretting. If we continue worrying about the problem and thinking about it, then we really do not believe.

When we shout in triumph, we are declaring that, by faith, we believe we already have the victory, and we are rejoicing because of that victory! A good example of this is in the following declaration:

> *We will **shout in triumph** at your salvation and victory, and in the name of our God we will set up our banners; the Lord will fulfill all our petitions. Now, I know that the Lord saves His anointed: He will answer him from His holy Heaven with the saving strength of His right hand. Some trust in and boast of chariots, and some of horses, but we will trust in and boast of the name of the Lord our God. They are bowed down and fallen; but we are risen and stand upright. O Lord, give victory; let the King answer us when we call.* (Ps. 20:5-9, AMP)

Here we see the declaration "we will shout in triumph" and "we will set up our banners." This is a declaration of faith before the answer is seen. When one sets up their banners, it is an indication that there has been victory after a battle. So they were shouting in triumph because they knew that by faith they had already won! God is speaking to the body of Christ today about the shout of victory, the shout of high praises to God, the shout of triumph! As the shout is restored to the Church, the gates of hell will **not** prevail against it. However, the church **shall** prevail against the gates of hell and shall see them come falling down. The Church shall overcome, prevail, and conquer!

Part of the covenant God made with Abraham, which we are to obtain through faith in Christ, is that we, as children of the seed of Abraham would possess the gates of **Our** enemies (Gen. 22:17). The "gates" stand for the power and defense. We are to **possess** the power of our enemies. Isaiah 60:18 says that we shall call our gates "Praise." In other words, our power is in praise, and our defense is in praise. Since we know that God **inhabits the praises of His people** (Ps. 22:3), we know that when God's presence comes, the power and the joy will come. We are also told that the gates of hell will not overcome or prevail against the Church. That means that the powers and defenses of the enemy will not be able to overcome the Church.

We are to rule and reign with Christ. He is coming back for a glorious Bride; an overcoming Bride—not a defeated one!

In fighting the battles, God has promised to be with us and to reward us while here on the earth.

Isaiah 45:2,3 (KJV) says:

I will go before thee and make the crooked places straight; I will break in pieces the gates of bronze

*and cut in sunder the bars of iron. I will give you
the treasures of darkness and hidden riches of
secret places, that you may know that I the Lord,
who call you by name, am the God of Israel.*

God has promised that He will go before us and
remove the problems and give us His blessings. First,
we must believe that He will do what He says He will
do. If God has promised to go before us and to remove
the problems, then why should we worry about them?
The only reason God has allowed them to come into our
lives is so that we may have the opportunity to overcome them through His strength. God does not allow
trials just to watch us become discouraged and to see us
be defeated. He allows them so that we can earn all the
blessings that are promised to those who overcome. God
has special rewards for those who overcome. (See Rev.
2:7,17,26; 3:5,12,21; 21:7). To the one who overcomes,
God has promised that we would be given to eat of the
tree of life and of hidden manna which is in the
paradise of God. It is the one who overcomes that will
sit with Him on His throne. It is the one who overcomes
that God will give a white stone with a new name written on it. To the one who overcomes and does God's will
to the end, He will give authority over the nations to
rule them. The one who overcomes will be dressed in
white and will never have his name erased from the
Book of Life. Those who overcome will be made a pillar
in the temple of God. We are told in Revelation 3:21,
NIV:

*To him who overcomes, I will give the right to sit
with me on my throne, just as I overcame and sat
down with my Father on his throne.*

The one who overcomes will inherit all things and God
will be called their Father and they will be called His son
and His daughter. To overcome, one must conquer and
master all obstacles. To overcome is to be victorious!

God would never allow us to go through anything that
He did not already have the answer for. He wants us to inherit all the blessings that one inherits who has overcome. He wants us to receive the Crown of Life that only
those who overcome will inherit. Without problems and
trials we would never have the opportunity to overcome!
So praise God for the trials!

The church is supposed to be victorious. We should be
on the offensive, **not** the defensive. We will not be overcome, but we shall overcome our enemy by the blood of
the Lamb and by the word of our testimony. Jesus conquered the devil, so now, in the midst of any kind of trial,
we are more than conquerors and gain a surpassing victory through Him who loved us. (Rom. 8:37)

Our testimony is this: "God is on my side. I have the
victory, for greater is the One that is in me than he who is
in the world. I am redeemed. I am healed. I am strong in
the power of His might. I have the mind of Christ. Jesus
is made unto me wisdom. I am the righteousness of God
in Him. I am above only and not beneath. Everything I set
my hands to do prospers." Hallelujah! Glory! Praise the
Lord!

And we have not seen **anything** yet! Wait until the Body of Christ, the army of God, begins fighting with the spiritual weapon of the SHOUT OF VICTORY!!! Just begin to shout down the obstacles in your way! Those mountains will become as flat land as you begin praising God for His mighty power to deliver you. Look what the Angel of the Lord said to Zerubbabel about the mountain that **seemed** to be in his way:

> *Then he answered and spake unto me, saying, This is the word of the Lord unto Zerubbabel, saying, not by might, nor by power, but by my Spirit saith the Lord of hosts. Who art thou, O great mountain? before Zerubbabel thou shalt become a plain: and he shall bring forth the headstone thereof **with SHOUTINGS**, crying **grace, grace** unto it. Moreover the word of the Lord came unto me, saying, The hands of Zerubbabel have laid the foundation of this house; his hands shall also finish it; and thou shalt know that the Lord of hosts hath sent me unto you. For who hath despised the day of small things? For they shall rejoice and shall see the plumb line the hand of Zerubbabel with those seven; they are the eyes of the Lord, which run to and fro through the whole earth.* (Zech. 4:6-10, KJV)

Zerubbabel was told to shout, "grace, grace" and the mountain would become as a plain. You see, God removes those mountains in our way by His Spirit and not by any of our carnal efforts. We can trust God to move in a mighty way on our behalf when we obey and fight the battles His way, through our shouting praises to Him!

Praise Jehovah Jireh, your provider. Praise El Shaddai, He's more than enough to meet your every need!! When you are in trouble, it is time to start SHOUTING.

I heard a story of a Christian lady who had been taught the ninety-first Psalm and told of God's power to protect her. She was accosted one night by a robber. She remembered to call upon God and began screaming and yelling, "Feathers! Feathers! Feathers!" That was the only word she could remember, but as she screamed out, "Feathers! Feathers! Feathers!" **her enemy fled.** Her loud yelling must have shocked and confused him, and in fear he ran away. Hallelujah!

I saw the power of High Praises overcome my strong enemy during the time I was president of a Christian women's group which met in a home for retired people. It was a beautiful building, and we had a lovely meeting room. God was sending many people who lived there to our meetings, and they were getting saved, filled with the Holy Spirit, and healed.

After a few months I learned of a man who had moved into the home who was a fortune teller. He had been predicting people's futures, even against their wills. Many of the people were being terrorized by him. He was even preventing some of the people from coming to our meetings through his threats.

One day, as I was walking toward the building, this man walked up to me and stood in front of me, preventing me from going any further. He put his face against mine and stated that he could "see through me." Then he began to predict my future. I tried to back away, but he grabbed my hand and held it tightly and continued his predictions. Everything happened so suddenly that my first reaction was fear. But I said to him, "I'm not afraid of you, and you have no power over me. Besides, you are a liar, satan, and the father of lies. I command you, in the Name of Jesus, to let me go." He continued his grip on my hand and said that he was more powerful than Jesus. I repeated several scriptures including, "Greater is He who is in me than he who is in you," but found myself becoming more and more frightened. Finally I began shouting praises (in tongues) to God, and suddenly he fell backward, almost as if I had hit him! He put his hands over his ears and cowered, saying "Don't say that! Don't say that!" and he got away from me as quickly as possible.

I stood there amazed at the look of fear on his face! That man ended up in the hospital within days with some kind of disease. He lost so much weight that we hardly recognized him when he got out of the hospital. Somehow he had lost his power to tell fortunes. No one was ever afraid of him again, nor did he ever again try to hinder anyone from coming to the meetings.

God inhabits the praises of his people. As we offer our praises to God, He comes on the scene. No devil can stay in the presence of Almighty God! Exodus 14:14 (KJV) reminds us:

The Lord shall fight for you and ye shall hold your peace.

We need to believe God is on our side and that He will surely fight our battles for us when we trust Him and refuse to fear. When Elisha and his servant were facing the vast army of horses and chariots who had surrounded them, Elisha told his servant:

Fear not; for those with us are more than those with them. Then Elisha prayed, Lord, I pray You, open his eyes that he may see. And the Lord opened the young man's eyes, and he saw; and behold, the mountain was full of horses and chariots of fire round about Elisha. (2 Ki. 6:17,18, AMP)

Sometimes we just need to pray and ask God to open our eyes to see the truth of the situation.

For He will give His angels (especial) charge over you, to accompany and defend and preserve you in all your ways (of obedience and service). They shall bear you upon their hands, lest you dash your foot against a stone. You shall tread upon the lion and adder, the young lion and the serpent shall you trample under foot. Because he has set his love upon Me, therefore will I deliver him; I will set him on high, because he knows and understands My name (has a personal knowledge of My mercy, love and kindness; trusts and relies on Me, knowing I will never forsake him, no, never.) He shall call upon me, and I will answer him; I will be with him in trouble, I will deliver him and honor him. With long life will

I satisfy him and show him my salvation. (Ps. 91:11-16, AMP)

Hallelujah! God has given His angels charge over you to protect you. He will never, never leave you! No matter what the circumstances, start praising Him for the victory. Receive it by faith, and then begin thanking the Lord for His goodness and mercy.

One of my favorite examples of shouting for the victory in battle is the story of King Jehoshaphat. The armies of Moab, Ammon, and Mount Seir, a great multitude, had joined together against him. When King Jehoshaphat heard about the vast army, he feared and set himself to seek the Lord. He proclaimed a fast throughout all Judah, and the people gathered together to ask the Lord for help. They cried out to Him, reminding God of His great might and power. Then they humbled themselves before God and reminded him of how insignificant and powerless they were against such an army. Finally, they said, "We don't know what to do, but we have our eyes upon You." As they were gathered together there, the Spirit of the Lord came upon the prophet Jahaziel. He prophesied:

*Hearken, all Judah, you inhabitants of Jerusalem and you King Jehoshaphat, the Lord says this to you: Be not afraid or dismayed at this great multitude; **for the battle is not yours but God's**. Tomorrow go down to them; behold, they will come up by the ascent of Zig; and you will find them at the end of the ravine before the wilderness of Jeruel. You shall not need to fight in this battle; take your*

position, stand still, and see the deliverance of the
Lord (Who is) with you, O Judah and Jerusalem.
Fear not, *nor be dismayed; tomorrow* ***go out***
against them *for the Lord is with you.* (2 Chr.
20:15-17, AMP)

Then Jehoshaphat and all Judah fell down on their
faces before the Lord, worshiping Him. And the others
stood up to praise the Lord with a very loud voice. The
next morning, as they went out, Jeshoshaphat exhorted
them, "Believe in the Lord your God, and you shall be established; believe and remain steadfast to His prophets,
and you shall prosper." Then he appointed singers to sing
to the Lord and praise Him in their holy (priestly) garments, as they went out before the army, saying, "Give
thanks to the Lord, for His mercy and loving kindness endure forever!" And when they began to sing and to praise,
the Lord set ambushes against the men of Ammon, Moab
and Mount Seir, who had come against Judah, and they
were self-slaughtered. Suspecting betrayal, the men of
Ammon and Moab rose against those of Mount Seir, utterly destroying them. And when they had made an end of
the men of Mount Seir, they all helped **destroy one**
another. And when Judah came to the watchtower of the
wilderness, they looked at the multitude, and behold,
there were dead bodies fallen to the earth, and none had
escaped! When Jehoshaphat and his people came to take
the spoil, they found among them much cattle, goods, garments, and precious things, which they took for themselves. There was more than they could carry away, so
much more that they were three days in gathering the

spoil! They had far more riches after the battle than they had before the battle began. God has a wonderful way of working all things together for the good of those who love and trust Him.

Notice in the above story that it was **when they began** singing and praising the Lord that He set ambushes against their enemies!

Often, it is after we have finished the battle that we have the rich experience of God's faithfulness to protect and to comfort us during the trial, and finally His mighty hand to deliver us! We can now enlarge the borders of our ministry as His ambassadors and comfort and encourage others with the same comfort we have received from God. For surely God's goodness and mercy shall **follow** us all the days of our lives!

We can say with David:

My lips will **shout** *for joy when I sing praises to Thee. And my soul, which Thou has redeemed.* (Ps. 71:23, NAS)

When you do not feel like shouting and praising the Lord as David did, shout for joy that God has redeemed your life from the hand of the enemy!

Nehemiah was a man who loved the Lord. God called Nehemiah to rebuild the house of the Lord. There were great shoutings and much praising the Lord as they built. Let's look at the story:

When the builders laid the foundation of the temple of the Lord, the priests stood in their vestments with trumpets, and the Levite sons of Asaph with their cymbals, to praise the LORD, after the order of David, King of Israel. They sang responsively, praising and giving thanks to the Lord, saying, For He is good, for His mercy and lovingkindness endure forever toward Israel. And all the people SHOUTED with a great shout when they praised the Lord, because the foundation of the house of the Lord was laid! But many of the priests and Levites and heads of fathers' houses, old men who had seen the first house (Solomon's temple), when the foundation of this house was laid before their eyes, wept with a loud voice, though many shouted aloud for joy; so the people could not distinguish the shout of joy from the sound of weeping of the people, for the people shouted with a loud shout and the sound was heard far off. (Ezra 3:10b, AMP)

Can you imagine, there was so much loud noise that the sound was heard far off? Now that is loud! Remember another time in history when the noise of God's people was heard far off?

On the day of Pentecost, there was **such a loud noise** that all the people of Jerusalem came out to see what was happening! Peter took the opportunity to preach the gospel to them, and there were added to God's Kingdom that day about three thousand souls. Glory to God!

Listen! Your watchmen lift up their voices. They SHOUT joyfully together, for they will see with their own eyes when the Lord restored Zion. Break forth, SHOUT joyfully together, you waste places of Jerusalem, for the Lord has comforted His people, He has redeemed Jerusalem. (Is. 52:8,9, NAS)

*Let thy priests be clothed with righteousness; let thy saints **SHOUT** for joy!* (Ps. 132:9, KJV)

And now my head will be lifted up above my enemies around me; and I will offer in His tent sacrifices with SHOUTS of joy; I will sing, yes, I will sing praises to the Lord. (Ps. 27:6, NAS)

*My lips will **SHOUT** for joy when I sing praises to Thee: and my soul, which Thou hast redeemed.* (Ps. 71:23, NAS)

*Thus all Israel brought up the ark of the covenant of the Lord with **SHOUTING**, and with the sound of the horn, with trumpets, with loud-sounding cymbals, with harps and lyres.* (1 Chr. 15:28, NAS)

***SHOUT** joyfully to the Lord, all the earth; break forth and sing for joy and sing praises.* (Ps. 98:4, NAS)

*We will **SHOUT** in triumph at your salvation and victory, and in the name of our God we will set up our banners; the Lord fulfill all your petitions.* (Ps. 20:5, AMP)

There are many other scriptures on shouting and crying out to God, and you can look them up for yourself. Most important of all, as His child, be a doer of the Word. Begin to sing and shout and rejoice in the Lord when the enemy comes around. The enemy remembers all down through history the times he has been defeated when God's people started rejoicing in the Lord and started SHOUTING and praising God. Let us restore the SHOUT of praise to our God! And as we see the time draw near to a close, we can look up, because our redemption draws near! Hallelujah!

*For the **Lord Himself shall descend from Heaven with a SHOUT,** with the voice of an archangel and with the trumph of God!* (1 Thess. 4:16, KJV)

Glory! Hallelujah! Praise the Lord! The LORD HIMSELF WILL SHOUT. And you better believe that the Body of Christ here on earth will **SHOUT** in return as they witness His coming!

VIII

Good Reason to Shout!

No matter how fierce the battle is we are going through, there are still many **good** reasons to SHOUT for joy. We can shout because our name is written in the Lamb's Book of Life. To have our name written in God's Book of Life means that we have an eternal home awaiting us in heaven. Jesus himself said that we should rejoice that our names are recorded in heaven. Jesus, who was God in the flesh, came down from heaven, lived among sinners, though he himself was sinless, and took upon Himself all of our filthy sins and bore them on the cross so that you and I might be able to be counted worthy to have our names written in the Book of Life and live forever in heaven with Him! What a wonderful Savior! No matter how good we are, we could never be good enough to be worthy of standing in the presence of a Holy God without the blood of Jesus making us worthy!

We are told in Luke 10:20 to "Rejoice because our names are written in heaven!" So we are to rejoice and shout praises to God for his goodness in choosing us to become children of God!

We can shout because God is **for** us and not against us.

What then shall we say to these things? If God is for us, who is against us? He who did not spare His own Son, but delivered Him up for us all, how will He not also with Him freely give us all things? Who will bring a charge against God's elect? God is the one who justifies; who is the one who condemns? Christ Jesus is He who died, yes, rather who was raised, who is at the right hand of God, who also intercedes for us. Who shall separate us from the love of Christ? Shall tribulation, or distress, or persecution, or famine, or nakedness, or peril, or sword? Just as it is written, "For Thy sake we are being put to death all day long; we were considered as sheep to be slaughtered." But in all these things we overwhelmingly conquer through Him who loved us; For I am convinced that neither death, nor life, nor angels, nor principalities, nor things present, nor things to come, nor powers, nor height, nor depth, nor any other created thing, shall be able to separate us from the love of God, which is in Christ Jesus our Lord. (Rom. 8:31-39, NAS)

When you are in distress, shout, "Praise God that this distress will **never** separate me from the love of God which is in Christ Jesus!" When in tribulation, shout, "Praise the Lord that this tribulation will **never** separate me from the love of God that is in Christ Jesus." Even if a loved one dies you can shout, "Praise God that this death shall not separate me from the Love of God which is in

Christ Jesus." No matter what happens in your life, you can still praise God for his love for you!

We can shout because our God has said:

I will never desert you, nor will I ever forsake you. So that we can confidently say, *the Lord is my helper, I will not be afraid. What shall man do to me?* (Heb. 13:5b-6, NAS)

We have a security that the world is longing and looking for. The unsaved do not have the confidence that God loves them and is with them no matter what is happening in their lives. Thank God that He has promised that He would not forsake us!

We can shout because it is written, the Lord is our help; He is our strength; He is our Rock; He is our shield, He is our fortress; He is our Light; He is our Salvation; He is our strong Tower; He is our refuge!

We can shout because of His great mercy and lovingkindness in providing the Blood of the Lamb that takes away **all** our sins! A one-time sacrifice, once and for all, our sins forgiven by God! He does not remember them anymore! They have been removed as far as the east is from the west! We can shout because though our sins were as scarlet, we have become as white as snow before the Lord!

There is therefore now no condemnation for those who are in Christ Jesus! (Rom. 8:1, NAS)

God's remedy for our sin was that, "He made Him who knew no sin (Jesus) to **be sin** on our behalf, that we might become the righteousness of God in Him. Now that is something to get excited and shout about! Say, "Praise you, sweet Jesus, for becoming sin for me. Thank you for taking all my sins on the cross so that I wouldn't be judged for them. Praise the LORD that I am righteous by faith!"

We can shout because He loves us so much that not only did He give Jesus to us as our Savior, but He has chosen us and has appointed us to go and to bear much fruit for His glory.

For God so loved the world, that He gave His only begotten Son, that, whoever believes in Him should not perish, but have eternal life. (John 3:16, NAS)

You did not choose Me, but I chose you, and appointed you, that you should go and bear fruit, and that your fruit should remain, that whatever you ask of the Father in My name, He may give to you. (John 15:16, NAS)

He has given us the honor of being called His children;

But as many as received Him, to them He gave the right to become children of God, even to those who believe in His name. (John 1:12, NAS)

He created us in **His** image. We are not created in the image of an ape or any other animal, no, we have been created in the very image of Almighty God! He formed us in our mother's womb.

For thou didst weave me in my mother's womb. I will give thanks to Thee, for I am fearfully and wonderfully made; Wonderful are Thy works, And my soul knows it very well. My frame was not hidden from Thee, when I was made in secret, and skillfully wrought in the depths of the earth. Thine eyes have seen my unformed substance and in Thy book they were all written, the days that were ordained for me, when as yet there was not one of them. (Ps. 139:13-16, NAS)

We can shout because we have been called into the ministry to be ambassadors for Christ.

*Therefore, if any man is in Christ, he is a new creature; the old things passed away; behold new things have come. Now all these things are from God, who reconciled us to Himself through Christ, and **gave us the ministry of reconciliation**, namely, that God was in Christ reconciling the world to Himself, not counting their trespasses against them, and He has committed to us the word of reconciliation. Therefore, we are **ambassadors for Christ**, as though God were entreating through us; we beg you on behalf of Christ, be reconciled to God.* (2 Cor. 5:17-20, NAS)

We can shout because we now have the mind of Christ.

For who has known the mind of the Lord, that he should instruct Him? But we have the mind of Christ. (1 Cor. 2:16, NAS)

And we can shout because we also have a strong sound mind.

For God has not given us a spirit of fear, but of power and of love and of a sound mind. (2 Tim. 1:7, NKJV)

Say, "Hallelujah! I have the mind of Christ, Thank you Father that you have given me the mind of Christ, Praise the name of the Lord that I don't have a spirit of fear anymore! Thank you Jesus that I have a **strong sound mind**! Hallelujah, Glory to God!"

We can be glad in the midst of trials and shout for joy because He has promised that He will turn all things together for the **good** for those who love Him and are called according to His purpose. Not only that, He has said that the trials would make us stronger, give us more patience and bring us to maturity! Hallelujah! Praise the Lord forever!

We can shout because He is our Good Shepherd. He will lead and guide us in our lives. We are promised that, as His sheep, we will **know** His voice and that He will provide all our needs according to His riches in Christ Jesus. So, He is our provider. When we have needs, we have the right to come boldly before His throne of grace and to obtain help. The righteous have never been found begging for bread, God has always provided for His own!

We can shout because He has promised to be our Healer.

And He said, "If you will give earnest heed to the voice of the Lord your God, and do what is right in His sight, and give ear to His commandments, and *keep all His statutes, I will put none of the diseases on you which I have put on the Egyptians; for I, the Lord, **am your healer.*** (Ex. 15:26, NAS)

He is **our healer**! God has told us that Jesus was punished; He suffered pain and agony so that we would not have to suffer. He was punished for our sins, He was wounded and pierced for our sickness, and because of His stripes, we are healed. We must believe that, and **receive** it! Begin shouting praises to God that He is your Great Physician!

We can shout because He has redeemed us, sanctified us, justified us, delivered us, etc. What more should I say? We have **so many** good reasons to shout our high praises to God. But the **best** reason is because He commands us to shout praises to Him!

O clap your hands all ye people and SHOUT unto God with the voice of triumph! (Ps. 47:1, KJV)

***SHOUT** for joy, O heavens, for the Lord has done it! SHOUT joyfully, you lower parts of the earth; break forth into a SHOUT of joy, you mountains, O forest, and every tree in it; for the Lord has redeemed Jacob and in Israel He shows forth His glory.* (Is. 44:23, NAS)

SHOUT for joy, O daughter of Zion! SHOUT in triumph, O Israel! Rejoice and exalt with all your heart, O daughter of Jerusalem! The Lord has taken away His judgments against you, He has cleared away your enemies. The King of Israel, the

Lord, is in your midst; you will fear disaster no more. (Zeph. 3:14,15, NAS)

Rejoice greatly, O daughter of Zion! SHOUT in triumph, O daughter of Jerusalem! Behold your King is coming to you. He is just and endowed with salvation. (Zech. 9:9, NAS)

Cry aloud and SHOUT for joy, O inhabitants of Zion for great in your midst is the Holy One of Israel. (Is. 12:6, NAS)

*Let them SHOUT for joy, and be glad, that favor my righteous cause; yea, let them say continually, let the Lord be magnified, which hath **pleasure** in the prosperity of his servant.* (Ps. 35:27, KJV)

There is also a practical reason to shout: when you are feeling tense and under stress, if you will begin to shout loud praises to God, you will find it releases all of the tension, stress, and pressure that you were experiencing. Shouting helps release the flowing of the Holy Spirit that is within us. You see, the Holy Spirit dwells in our belly.

He that believeth on me, as the scriptures hath said, out of his belly shall flow rivers of living water. (John 7:38, KJV)

The Holy Spirit who dwells in our innermost being or "belly" is released as we shout and comes flowing out as rivers of living water.

Therefore with joy shall ye draw waters out of the wells of salvation. (Is. 12:3, KJV)

I want to share some wonderful examples of God answering prayers because of people shouting High Praises to the Lord. Last spring, I was in California on a speaking tour. I was teaching on the power of shouting high praises to God. At a certain meeting I felt strongly impressed in my spirit to tell the people that too often we accept things as God's will and give up on our prayers when the truth is: what happened was not really God's will at all.

I talked about taking authority over the devil and doing spiritual warfare. As the Holy Spirit moved, faith started to rise in the people's hearts. I sensed that there were people there who had been praying for many, many years but had not had breakthroughs. At the close of the meeting, I asked everyone there to get up from their seats and to begin thanking God for the breakthroughs. We had a glorious time of shouting together, and, as we left, everyone felt encouraged and lifted up.

Many times I never hear what happens after I am gone from a place, but about six weeks later, a lady from that city called me at my home and said that she just had to get in contact with me because she was so excited about the answers to prayer that she and her friends who had attended that meeting were experiencing.

She told me that after I left, she and others would meet together, and listen to my tape, then they would "do it." I said, "Do what?" She answered, "SHOUT, of course!" She shared that she had an answer to a prayer that she had been praying for thirty-five years! She said that they had been experiencing tremendous breakthroughs and answers to their prayers.

I asked her to share with me the answer to the prayer that she had been praying for some thirty-five years. She told me the story of how her son who was three-and-a-half years old at the time had been abducted from her by a man and woman. She had spent all these years crying and begging God to help her find her son. She told the Lord, "How can a mother forget her son? I will never have peace until you let me find him!" She told me that as she was shouting, she began realizing that she had accepted this as God's will and had never really taken authority over the devil. As she took authority over the devil, she **knew** that she had the victory and began laughing at the devil, knowing that he could not hold her son in darkness anymore.

To make a very long story short, she was reunited with her son shortly after that! Not only that, but all the years she had been praying for him about his school days, his marriage, etc., God had been answering her prayers, and her son was a beautiful Christian and had married a wonderful Christian girl. He had a child who he had named after his mother as he had remembered her name. He too, had been praying for years to be restored to his real mother. God answered their prayers very miraculously and reunited them! It was a glorious reunion! PRAISE THE LORD FOREVER! Hallelujah!

May God be glorified through her witness and testimony. I pray that the Lord will open many doors for this lady to share her testimony and that in sharing how faithful God is, it will encourage many of His children. The day she called me, I was a little discouraged, and it really encouraged me and brought me out of the attack of oppression I was in. God is so good, He knows just what we need!

How I wish I had kept a notebook over the years of all the times that God has answered prayers. There have been thousands of prayers answered! When we are going through a trial or testing, we need to look back and to **remember** all the answered prayers and how faithful God has been. Each one of us could share many testimonies of His goodness. The enemy would have us forget those past victories, since just recalling God's faithfulness in times past will encourage us and increase our faith. We should always share the wonderful answers to prayer with each other, for it is written that we shall overcome the enemy by the "word of our testimony" and by the "blood of the Lamb!"

IX

The Shout of a King

Last year I was planning a speaking tour to the West Coast. I had intended to speak on the subject of "shouting," when I received several calls from various cities where I would be speaking. Each one warned me of the spiritual battle taking place in their city and of the witchcraft, new age movement, divination, and curses being put upon the Christians. After several of these phone calls, I began to feel like I was not too certain that I really wanted to go to California at all! And especially travel alone! Fear began to grip my heart as I heard stories of past preachers who the enemy had devoured!

I began inquiring of the Lord, asking Him, was He certain that I was strong enough in Him to go into this battleground? As I sought the Lord for the answer, He took me to the book of Numbers, chapter 23, for the answer.

In Numbers 23, we find the story of King Balak, an enemy of the children of Israel, who saw them coming out of Egypt toward the promised land. He was afraid, so he called for the prophet Balaam and tried to get him to speak curses against God's children. Balaam realized God had blessed the children of Israel and that he could not curse them. Instead, he blessed them. Then Balak said, "I told you to curse them, but you blessed them altogether." And Balaam said, "God is not a man that He should lie." He realized God had already blessed Israel and would not go back on His word. He had a covenant with them, and it was a covenant of blessings, not cursing. He said, "Behold, I have received a commandment to bless and cannot reverse it." He went on to say, "The Lord his God is with them and the **shout of a King** is among them." There was a shout of a King among God's children, and Balaam was not able to curse them. Hallelujah!

When the King shouts, he's shouting praises, because he has just won the battle! There was **already** the shout of a King among the people of God. It wasn't shouts to their earthly King though. Up to this time in the history of Israel they had no Kings. They were shouting to their "King of Kings, and Lord of Lords," the "Almighty God!" Despite the fact that they had no earthly King, they had the faith and confidence to know and to believe that their "King of Kings" was with them. They were shouting because they realized they had already won the battle!

Because God inhabits our praises, He was there when the children of Israel were praising Him. He was their Shield, and **NO ONE COULD PUT ANY KIND OF A CURSE ON THEM!** God had pronounced a blessing upon His children, and no one had the power or authority to reverse it. Not even the prophet Baalam, and he knew that.

The Lord showed me very clearly through this account in Numbers that, as His child, I did not need to be afraid of any curse, witchcraft, divination, hex, spell, etc., that any evil person tried to put on me. As long as I was shouting high praises to my King, THE DEVIL COULD NOT TOUCH ME! Not only that, The Lord told me to speak out loud every day and to proclaim "THE DEVIL CAN'T TOUCH ME!"

That trip I took to California was very successful! God did great and mighty things! People came to the Lord, many were healed, delivered and encouraged in their faith. There was great victory everywhere I went. I am so glad that I did not let fear keep me from going where God wanted me to minister. The Lord had once again confirmed to me the importance of giving Him thanks in all things. He had been my shield and strength!

It is the same today for all God's children. God **always** inhabits our praises. He is our Mighty Shield, and there is no kind of witchcraft or curse that anyone can put on one of God's children upon whom He has pronounced a blessing, who are walking in His Spirit, giving Him thanks, and praising Him in everything.

We have a King who has already won the battle, and He lives on the inside of us. He wants to shout praises through us because He knows that we are victorious through Him.

Let there be a shout of a King among God's people today. Let us restore the shout as we see the days drawing near to our King's soon return. For the Lord Himself

shall "descend with a SHOUT, with the voice of the arch-angel, and with the trumpet of God." Jesus is going to return with a shout! The head never does anything apart from the body. The children of God shall be shouting when we see the heavens open up and our King riding on a white horse.

Let the lips of a people who believe their God shout for joy and rejoice at His soon return! Let us **Shout for the victory** because the battle is not ours, but God's. He shall fight for us, for He always causes us to triumph through Christ Jesus. Amen! even so, Come Lord Jesus!

I will go before you and make the rough places smooth; I will shatter the doors of bronze and cut through their iron bars. (Is. 45:2, NAS)

These scriptures and others like them teach that God is the one causing the victories and defeats on the earth; that battles lost or won on earth are the result of those lost or won in the heavenlies between the good and the bad angels. Over every kingdom of this world, there are good and bad spirits who seek to carry out the will of their master.

We see in the account of Daniel where Daniel was praying and fasting and seeking God. After many days, the angel Gabriel came to him and told Daniel that from the **first** day he had sought God, He had heard him and had sent Gabriel to answer his prayer. But Gabriel had been detained for twenty-one days by a heavenly prin-cipality, with whom Gabriel had been fighting, until

Michael, one of the chief princes of heaven, came to help him.

If Daniel had given up in discouragement during those days of waiting and praying, he would never have been able to have had the encounter with the angel Gabriel, let alone have his prayer answered.

So often, there is a heavenly battle going on during our time of waiting, and we fail to persevere because we think that maybe God has not heard our prayer or has decided not to answer our prayer. We do not continue to pray in faith with perseverance, not realizing that there is a heavenly battle going on, and we often give up, thus allowing the enemy to win the battle.

We are instructed by the Lord:

Cast not away therefore your confidence, which hath great recompence of reward. FOR YE HAVE NEED OF PATIENCE, that after ye have done the will of God, ye might receive the promise. For yet a little while, and he that shall come will come and will not tarry. Now the just shall live by faith; but if any man draw back, my soul shall have no pleasure in him. But we are not of them who draw back unto perdition; but of them that believe to the saving of the soul. (Heb. 10:35, KJV)

It would be so much easier if we could see this heavenly battle going on around us. Then we surely would take spiritual things more seriously! Can you imagine what it would be like if God would allow us to see this invisible battle? I WOULD IMAGINE THAT IF FOR JUST ONE DAY OF OUR ENTIRE LIFE WE SAW THE REAL BATTLE, IT WOULD CHANGE US FOR THE REST OF OUR LIVES. WE WOULD NO LONGER LIVE OUR LIVES UNWISELY, WASTING TIME, BUT WE WOULD BE AWARE OF THE DAILY NEED TO CONSTANTLY BE IN PRAYER, SUPPLICATION, FASTING, PRAISE, SHOUTING, AND ANY OTHER THING THAT WE COULD THINK OF TO GET THE VICTORY. LET THERE BE A SHOUT FOR THE KING AMONG GOD'S PEOPLE!

As long as we are in faith and praising and thanking God for the victory, the devil will not be able to defeat us. Every day we should be celebrating the goodness of the Lord. We should be exulting in God our Savior who has done great and mighty things for us. We should be shouting praises to Him for all the battles that are won by faith, knowing that we shall soon see the answer. For He is faithful who has promised it!

X

A Mighty Roar!

*The Lord **ROARS** from Zion, and thunders from Jerusalem; the pastures of the shepherds mourn, and the top of Carmel withers. (Amos 1:2, NIV)*

*The Lord will **ROAR** from Zion, and **thunder** from Jerusalem; the earth and the sky will tremble. But the Lord will be a refuge for His people, a stronghold for the people of Israel. (Joel 3:16, NIV)*

*They shall follow the Lord; He will **ROAR** like a lion. When He **ROARS**, His children will come trembling from the west. (Hos. 11:10, NIV)*

*He will lift up a banner to the nations from afar, and will whistle to them from the ends of the earth; surely they shall come with speed, swiftly. No one will be weary or stumble among them, no one will slumber or sleep; nor will the belt on their loins be loosed, nor the strap of their sandals be broken; whose arrow are sharp, and all their bows bent; their horses' hooves will seem like flint, and their wheels like a whirlwind. Their **ROARING** will be*

*like a lion, they will **ROAR** like young lions; yes,
they will **ROAR** and lay hold of the prey; they will
carry it away safely, and no one will deliver. In that
day they will **ROAR** against them like the **ROAR-
ING** of the sea. And if one looks to the land behold,
darkness and sorrow; and the light is darkened by
the clouds.* (Isa. 5:26-30, NKJ)

The original Hebrew word for the word roar was
"rumble" or "to mightily roar," "to make a loud sound, in
great commotion or tumult," "to rage, war, moan,
clamor—cry out aloud, be troubled, make in tumult,
tumultuous, be in an uproar."

In the above scriptures, we are told that the Lord shall
roar out of Zion! He will roar against His enemies! The
Almighty God is gathering His Church together in these
last days and exposing the deceptions of the enemy. His
people are beginning to rise up with a mighty indignation
against their enemy. They are putting their foot down and
saying "no more of this satan, I've had enough, I rebuke
you in the Mighty name of Jesus Christ. I come against
you with the Blood of the Lamb of God and the word of my
testimony. My testimony is that you are a defeated foe.
You were defeated at the cross of Calvary once and for all!
Jesus triumphed over you and made an open display of
you. You will bow your knees at the Mighty name of
Jesus!"

Our enemy, the devil, prowls around like a roaring lion
looking for someone to devour. He is on the offensive, har-
rassing God's children unrelentlessly. But it is time that
we get on the offensive and roar right back at him! As the

children of the Almighty, we need to rise up and fight. We need to be on the offensive and not on the defensive. This is warfare and we are not going to win without a fight. The Body of Christ must join forces and take an **unrelenting offensive position** against our enemy much like the example of the recent Persian Gulf war.

On January 15, 1991 President George Bush with the backing of allied partners ordered an air attack against the forces of Iraq for the unjust invasion of Kuwait under the leadership of Suddam Hussein.

The allied forces were well prepared and at the time they planned for war there was **no** hesitation or waiting to see if the enemy would fire the first bomb.

They started the war at the precise time as planned. The allied troops went in on the offensive **unlike** the Vietnam War when the United States took the defensive position and eventually lost the war, returning home in defeat.

Because of the unrelenting offensive position taken by the allied forces, there was a great victory as they moved forward to push back enemy forces.

There was total unity and cooperation between the United States and the other nations fighting Iraq. They had a common goal—to WIN THE WAR. They refused to quit until they realized complete and total victory.

At the United States Military Academy, General H. Norman Schwarzkopf, the commander of allied forces of the Persian Gulf War, was quoted as saying, "We knew that we were going up against a genuinely evil man."

As soldiers of the army of God, we too are having our eyes opened up to see that there is an evil force in the world. Our commander in chief—the Lord of Hosts—is sounding a trumpet call to war.

The army of God is rising up against their enemy as never before. They are putting on their armor of God and going forth to take the land away from satan and to divide the spoils. The Church of God will be a MIGHTY OVER-COMING CHURCH! A Church who is on the offensive not the defensive!

When we see the little ones of God being tossed around, we will come to their aid and help them in the battle. We will no longer be judging or criticizing each other. We will no longer fall into that trap of the devil. But we will walk together in love and in unity as never before. As we join hands together to fight against the devil instead of each other, a dynamite power will come forth that will not be able to stop or to defeat us!

Blow the trumpet in Zion, and sound an alarm in My holy mountain! Let all the inhabitants of the land tremble; for the day of the Lord is coming, for it is at hand: A day of darkness and gloominess, a day of clouds and thick darkness, like the morning clouds spread over the mountains. A people come, great and strong, the like of whom has never been; nor will there ever be any such after them, even for many successive generations. **A FIRE DEVOURS BEFORE THEM,** *and behind them a flame burns; the land is like the Garden of Eden before them, and behind them a desolate wilderness; surely nothing* *shall escape them. Their appearance is like the appearance of horses; and like swift steeds, so they run. With a noise like chariots over mountaintops they leap, like the noise of a flaming fire that devours the stubble, like a strong people set in battle array. Before them the people writhe in pain; all faces are drained of color. They run like a mighty men, they climb the wall like* **MEN OF WAR;** *every one marches in formation, And they do not break ranks. They do not push one another; every one marches in his own column. And when they lunge between the weapons, they are not cut down. They run to and fro in the city, they run on the wall; they climb into the houses, they enter at the windows like a thief. The earth quakes before them, the heavens tremble; the sun and moon grow dark, and the stars diminish their brightness. The Lord gives voice before His army, for His camp is very great; for strong is the One who executes His word. For the day of the Lord is great and very terrible; who can endure it? "Now, therefore," says the Lord, "turn to Me with all your heart, with fasting, with weeping, and with mourning." So rend your heart, and not your garments; return to the Lord your God, for He is gracious and merciful, slow to anger, and of great kindness; and He relents from doing harm. Who knows if He will turn and relent, and leave a blessing behind Him—a grain offering and a drink offering for the Lord your God? Blow the trumpet in Zion, consecrate a fast, call a sacred assembly;*

117

*gather the people, sanctify the congregation, as-
semble the elders, gather the children and nursing
babes; let the bridegroom go out from his chamber,
and the bride from her dressing room. Let the
priests, who minister to the Lord, weep between the
porch and the altar; let them say, "Spare your
people, O Lord, and do not give your heritage to
reproach, that the nations should rule over them."
Why should they say among the peoples, "Where is
their God?" Then the Lord will be zealous for His
land, and pity His people. The Lord will answer
and say to His people, "Behold, I will send you
grain and new wine and oil, and you will be satisfied by them; I will no longer make you a reproach
among the nations. But I will remove far from you
the northern army, and will drive him away into a
barren and desolate land, with his face toward the
eastern sea and his back toward the western sea;
His stench will come up, and his foul odor will rise,
because he has done monstrous things." Fear not, O
land; be glad and rejoice, for the Lord has done
marvelous things! Do not be afraid, you beasts of
the field; for the open pastures are springing up,
and the tree bears its fruit; the fig tree and the vine
yield their strength. Be glad then, you children of
Zion, and rejoice in the Lord your God; for He has
given you the former rain faithfully, and He will
cause the rain to come down for you—the former
rain, and the latter rain in the first month. The
threshing floors shall be full of wheat, and the vats*

shall overflow with new wine and oil. So I will re-
store to you the years that the swarming locust has
eaten, the crawling locust, the consuming locust,
and the chewing locust, My great army which I sent
among you. You shall eat in plenty and be satisfied,
and praise the name of the Lord your God, who has
dealt wondrously with you; and My people shall
never be put to shame. Then you shall know that I
am in the midst of Israel, and that I am the Lord
your God and there is no other. My people shall
never be put to shame. And it shall come to pass
afterward that I will pour out my Spirit on all flesh;
your sons and your daughters shall prophesy, your
old men shall dream dreams, your young men shall
see visions; and also on My menservants and on my
maidservants I will pour out my Spirit in those
days. And I will show wonders in the heavens and
in the earth: Blood and fire and pillars of smoke.
The sun shall be turned into darkness, and the
moon into blood, before the coming of the great and
terrible day of the Lord. And it shall come to pass
that whoever calls on the name of the Lord shall be
saved. For in Mount Zion and in Jerusalem there
shall be deliverance, as the Lord has said, among
the remnant whom the Lord calls. (Joel 2, NKJV)

Jesus, when He comes back, is not coming back as the
"Lamb of God." He is coming back as "The Mighty Warrior" and the "Lion of the Tribe of Judah." He is coming
back to declare war against His enemies. The day of God's
vengeance will come! Jesus is preparing His army on

earth to fight the battle with Him. We are being prepared to rule and to reign with Jesus.

The Lord is known throughout scripture as a "Man of War." Until recently, the body of Christ has missed this part of the character of God. We have learned much about the God of Love and the God of Mercy, but now it is time for us to learn about the "Man of War." Moses knew God as his Mighty Warrior, and he called Him that in Exodus 15:3 (KJV).

*The Lord is a **man of war**; the Lord is His name.*

David knew God as the God who taught his hands to war:

*He teaches my hands to **make war**, so that my arms can bend a bow of bronze.* (Ps. 18:34, NKJV)

*Blessed be the Lord my Rock, who trains my hands for **war** and my fingers for battle.* (Ps. 144:1, NKJV)

Isaiah knew the Lord as a **man of war**:

*The Lord will go forth like a **warrior**, He will arouse his zeal like a **man of war**. He will utter a **SHOUT**, yes, He will raise a **WAR CRY**, he will prevail against His enemy.* (Is. 42:13, NAS)

When Jesus was here on the earth, the zeal for the house of the Lord consumed Him with an intense passionate righteous anger. That zeal for His Father's house caused Jesus to go into the temple and to cast out all those who were buying and selling and to overturn the tables of the moneychangers and the seats of those who were selling doves. He made a scourge of cords and drove them out of the temple. When Jesus saw sin and injustice, He became angry. His anger was a godly, righteous anger. That same zeal for the Lord's house is beginning to be poured out on His body of believers and consume them.

When we see sin and injustice, it should effect us in the same way as it did Jesus. We should rise up with a holy, righteous anger and confront it. If it is demonic, then we need to get angry with the devil and declare war against him! When he comes as a roaring lion, we need to roar right back at him and fight him to the end.

*Therefore, prophesy against them all these words, and say to them: "The Lord will **ROAR** from on high, and utter His voice from His holy habitation; He will **ROAR** mightily against his fold, He will give a **SHOUT**, as those who tread the grapes, against all the inhabitants of the earth. A noise will come to the ends of the earth—for the Lord has a controversy with the nations; He will plead His case with all flesh, He will give those who are wicked to the sword, says the Lord."* (Jer. 25:30-31, NKJV)

As God's Ambassadors, who represent "The Almighty One," we are to prophesy against the evil, even **SHOUT** against it! We are to be His mouthpiece in the earth and to warn the people of the soon coming day of the Lord. The day of vengeance of our God. A very great and terrible day. A great day for the children of God, but a terrible day for the unbeliever. Great for the children of God because we are going to behold our Commander-and-Chief in all His glory and array. It will be a glorious day for the believer! But a terrible day for the heathen; they will dread seeing Him. Terror will strike their hearts as they realize that God is now their enemy and that they have no more chance to repent!

Already, days of darkness are coming upon the world as we approach the second coming of our Messiah, Jesus Christ. In this decade of the nineties, there will be much economical confusion among the nations and peoples. There will be more sickness and unheard-of-diseases, which are the latter day plagues coming upon the earth. People will live in fear and dread because of the chaos. There will be much spiritual darkness as we see the occult spreading; everything from satanism to New Age, humanism etc. Many will be deceived and lead others astray. There will be more and more false prophets and false teachers introducing destructive heresies, even in the church, denying Jesus Christ, deceiving even the elect of God, especially those who are not grounded firmly in the Word of God.

One pastor says, "It will be the best of times and the worst of times." The best of times for the people of God who are strong in faith and the Word of God. But the worst of times for the lukewarm and heathen, as they are tossed about by every wind of doctrine. They will not have the answers to the disaster and destruction, fear and poverty etc. There will be much turmoil among the unbelievers. But for the Church, there will be much opportunity to witness as never before. There will be a great end-time harvest such as the church has never known before.

*Arise, shine, for your light has come and the glory of the Lord has risen upon you. For behold darkness will cover the earth, and deep darkness the peoples; but the Lord will rise upon you, and His glory will appear upon you. And nations will come to your light, and kings to the brightness of your rising. Lift up your eyes round about, and see; they all gather together, they come to you. Your sons will come from afar, and your daughters will be carried in the arms. Then you will see and be radiant, and your heart will thrill and rejoice; because the abundance of the sea will be turned to you. The wealth of the nations will come to you. A multitude of camels will cover you, the young camels of Median and Ephah; all those from Sheba will come; they will bring gold and frankincense, and will **bear good news of the praises of the Lord**. All the flocks of Kedar will be gathered together to you. The rams of Nebaioth will minister to you; They will go up with acceptance on My altar, **And I shall glorify My glorious house**.* (Is. 60:1-8, NAS)

God's house will be glorified and lifted up before the world! The children of God will become stronger and bolder in the Lord as never before. They will be the only one with the answers to the world's problems! It is time to stir up the Spirit within us and to call forth that mighty warring Spirit of the Lord. It is time to let God arise within us and His enemies be scattered! It is time to allow the Lord God to ROAR out of Zion, His holy people.

*Indeed, (at His thunderings) my heart also trembles, and leaps out of its place. Hear, oh, hear the **roar of His voice** and the sound of rumbling that goes out of His mouth! Under the whole heaven He lets it loose, and His lightning to the ends of the earth. After it His voice **roars**; He thunders with the voice of His majesty, and He restrains not (His lightnings against His adversaries) when His voice is heard. God thunders marvelously with His voice; He does great things which we cannot comprehend.* (Job 37:1-5, AMP)

The voice of the Lord is not weak and faint. The voice of the Lord is mighty like a great thunder. The voice of the Lord is majestic and awesome. At the voice of the Lord, His enemies shall tremble and scatter!

Psalm 18 will help you get an idea of His voice, how mighty and great it is:

In my distress I called to the Lord; I cried to my God for help. From His temple he heard my voice; my cry came before Him, into His ears. The earth trembled and quaked, and the foundations of the mountains shook; they trembled because he was angry. Smoke rose from His nostrils; consuming fire came from His mouth, burning coals blazed out of it. He parted the heavens and came down; dark clouds were under His feet. He mounted the cherubim and flew; He soared on the wings of the wind. He made darkness His covering, His canopy around Him—the dark rain clouds of the sky. Out of the brightness of

His presence clouds advanced, with hailstones and bolts of lightning. The Lord thundered from heaven; the voice of the Most High resounded. He shot His arrows and scattered the enemies, great bolts of lightning and routed them. The valleys of the sea were exposed and the foundations of the earth laid bare at your rebuke, O Lord, at the blast of breath from your nostrils. He reached down from on high and took hold of me; He drew me out of deep waters. He rescued me from my powerful enemy, from foes, who were too strong for me. They confronted me in the day of my disaster, but the Lord was my support. He brought me out into a spacious place; He rescued me because He delighted in me. (Ps. 18:6-19, NIV)

We have a King who is our Victorious Warrior. HE IS ON OUR SIDE! He has already won the battle and is well able to win **ANY** battle in the future. He lives on the inside of us. Allow Him to shout forth praises of victory. He knows that we are victorious through Him. We need to know that we know that He is the Mighty Warrior living on the inside of us! Not only that, but it is written:

The Lord your God is in your midst, a victorious warrior. He will exult over you with joy, He will be quiet in His love, He will rejoice over you with SHOUTS of joy. (Zep. 3:17, NAS)

Even so, **ROAR**, O Lion of Judah! Rise up you children of God and **ROAR**, Yes, **SHOUT FOR THE VICTORY!**

About the Author

Judith Reno is an anointed and unique gift to the Body of Christ. Baptized with the Holy Spirit in 1975, she has been a delight and inspiration to all that have come into contact with her. Her openness and approachable nature, as well as her stirring testimonies of God's miraculous answers to prayers will bring great encouragement and stability to those who hear her teach. In this time of great outpourings of God's miraculous power upon the earth, Judith stands thoroughly yielded as a vessel for the working of His miracles.

As a teacher, Judith has done extensive studies on prayer, fasting, spiritual warfare, worship, the character of God, family relationships and the woman believer as well as many other topics. At the time she was baptized in the Holy Spirit, God spoke to her. "I have ordained you and called you to feed my sheep." Since that time it has been her intense desire to study the Word of God and to teach His wonderful truths.

As a evangelist, Judith is fluent in all the gifts of the Holy Spirit and has the ability to encourage believers to great exploits in the name of Jesus as they receive the impartation of who they are in Christ. The Lord has given her the unique gift of allowing her to "reap the harvest where others have labored" and she has been blessed to reap the benefits of their labors. (John 4:38)

Her experience as a pastor brings much insight into the heart and mercy of God. The wisdom of God is upon her as she brings forth counsel from the simplest to the most complex of situations. Her ability to bring forth "fresh manna" from the throne room as well as her ability to dispense His Word in practical everyday applications, feeds and inspires the Body of Christ to become all that God has ordained them to be for His glory.

The Lord has anointed her as a prophetess to His people especially in the area of "Prophetic prayers" as His Spirit directs. Judith has a special anointing that will ignite, stir and set ablaze the Spirit of God within you. The Lord has used her to heal the broken hearted and set the captive free.

The Lord has used her in "new beginnings" of several ministries, including founder and first president of *Woman Aglow* in Reston, Virginia. She and her husband Fred were founders and co-pastors of "House of Prayer Ministries." They also founded "Couples for Christ," an outreach ministry to reach couples for Christ, bringing healing and restoration to troubled marriages, and to give couples a vision for ministering together "hand in hand."

Judith has ministered nationally as well as internationally in Europe and the Middle East. She has spoken at various churches, retreats, conferences, Woman Aglow and other woman's ministries. She also teaches on "Redeeming Woman," a Northern Virginia cable television program.

She is author of the book *Shout for the Victory* and *The Fervent Prayers of a Righteous Woman Availeth Much!*, a workbook on the power of prayer.

Judith has been married 26 years and has two daughters and a granddaughter. As a graduate of Word of Faith Bible School, she is licensed and ordained by Buddy Harrison of Faith Christian Fellowship in Tulsa, Oklahoma.

Speaking Engagements
or
Teaching Seminars

Judith Reno is available for seminars or other speaking engagements throughout the year for churches, conferences and retreats.

Judith and her husband, Fred, are available also to minister to couples, groups, churches, conferences and seminars.

Subjects included are Prayer, Fasting, Spiritual Warfare, Marriage and Family, Developing Leaders and General Bible Teaching.

Please Contact:

**House of Prayer Ministries
P.O. Box 2725
Fairfax, VA 22031**

**Would Your Friends Enjoy
Receiving These
Books as a Gift From You?**

ORDER FORM

Send me (_____) copies of *Shout for the Victory* at $6.95 per copy (plus $2 shipping). $_____

Send me (_____) copies of the workbook, *The Fervent Prayers of a Righteous Man Availeth Much!* at $10.95 per copy (plus $2 shipping). $_____

Subtotal	$_____
Shipping	$_____
Total	$_____

Ship my order to:

First, Last Name_____

Street_____

City, State_____

Zip Code_____

Please allow 2 to 3 weeks for delivery

Send this form and check to:

HOUSE OF PRAYER MINISTRIES
P.O. Box 2725
Fairfax, VA 22031

Please send me
the following tape(s):

_____ @ $5.00, plus
                                $1.00 shipping $_____

_____ @ $5.00, plus
                                $1.00 shipping $_____

_____ @ $5.00, plus
                                $1.00 shipping $_____

                                   Subtotal $_____
                                   Shipping $_____
                                   Total $_____

Ship my order to:

First, Last Name_____

Street_____

City, State_____

Zip Code_____

Please allow 2 to 3 weeks for delivery

Send this form and check to:

**HOUSE OF PRAYER MINISTRIES
P.O. Box 2725
Fairfax, VA 22031**